THUNDER

GIVING THE GAME AWAY

Cover designed by Paul Tippett for Vitamin P
Book designed by Paul Tippett and Adrian Andrews for Vitamin P

Photographs supplied by: The Bowes family, the Morley family, the Aitken family, the Matthews family,
the Childs family, Marty Moffatt, Jason Joyce, George Chin, PG Brunelli/IconicPix, Paul Rider,
Midori Tsukagoshi, Charlie Best, Andrew Linden, Andy Earl, Jill Furmanovsky/rockarchive.com,
Glen LaFerman, Simon Fowler, Phil Nicholls, Paul Tippett, CBW/Alamy Stock Photo, WENN Ltd/Alamy
Stock Photo, Shutterstock. Every effort has been made to trace the copyright holders of the photographs
in this book but one or two were unreachable. We would be grateful if the photographers concerned
would contact us.

ISBN: 978.1.78558.137.3
Order No: OP56661

Exclusive Distributors
Music Sales Limited,
14/15 Berners Street,
London, W1T 3LJ.

Music Sales Pty Ltd
Level 4
30-32 Carrington St
Sydney
NSW 2000
Australia

Printed in Malta.

A catalogue record for this book is available from the British Library.

Visit Omnibus Press on the web at www.omnibuspress.com

THUNDER

GIVING THE GAME AWAY

TONITRUA · MADE IN · ENGLAND · IMPERAT

FORTIS · ET MAGNA

THE OFFICIAL BIOGRAPHY
JOEL McIVER

OMNIBUS PRESS

London / New York / Paris / Sydney / Copenhagen / Berlin / Madrid / Tokyo

THIS BOOK IS DEDICATED TO OUR FANS AND FAMILIES.
THANK YOU FOR PUTTING UP WITH OUR UNHOLY
RACKET FOR SO LONG...

CONTENTS

FOREWORD

SOME OF THE GREATEST MUSIC I EVER RECORDED, AND SOME OF THE GREATEST HANGOVERS I EVER SUFFERED, HAPPENED WHEN I WAS WITH THUNDER.

To produce a Thunder album, as I did with their first record back in 1990, you need to be pretty fit; you need to have a large liver; and you need to have a deep love of rock. You can't fake rock music: it's not pop. The rock audience won't let you off that easy. It's about trust: you're not marketing to them. They've either got you, or they ain't.

Thunder achieved what most people never, ever get to achieve. They've got something out of this business and it hasn't left them potless and fucked up. That's what I always admired about Thunder: they were smart guys, not cokeheads who messed about. They were professionals, and that professionalism is what's carrying them now. They were mates, too: the bond between them goes back a long, long way, and nothing will break that. They have an unbreakable friendship and respect for each other. It's who they are, and where they come from.

Hand on heart, working with those guys was the most fun I ever had recording a band in the UK. Look what we created... and the fuckers are still going. Thunder are playing arenas – I'm not. (Then again, I don't have to!)

Andy Taylor
Producer, songwriter, sometime Duran Duran guitarist, lighter thief and bon vivant

INTRODUCTION

WRITING THUNDER'S OFFICIAL MEMOIR IS VERY MUCH LIKE MAKING LOVE TO A BEAUTIFUL WOMAN, AS SWISS TONI WOULD HAVE IT. YOU LISTEN TO THEM DRONE ON FOR HOURS AND HOURS BEFORE THEY LET YOU ENTER THEIR INNER SANCTUM (THE MANAGEMENT OFFICE), WHIP OUT YOUR SAMSUNG (A DICTAPHONE) AND SQUEEZE THE ESSENTIAL INFORMATION INTO A TIGHT SPACE (THE PAGES OF THIS BOOK... WHICH COULD EASILY HAVE BEEN TWICE AS LONG).

It's been fun. In fact it's been a lot of fun. Over the months of interviews that went into *Giving The Game Away: The Official Biography*, I've heard tales from the horse's mouth that would make your nose-hair curl. In the three decades and more that the various members, ex-members and associates of Thunder have been making music and generally avoiding getting a haircut and a proper job, they've worked their way through lakes of booze and armies of 'post-gig companions', butting heads with a vivid crowd of music-industry types of varying levels of trustworthiness along the way. Most of these gory episodes have made it into this book, although some of the sauciest revelations have been omitted in the interests of good taste, and also because I don't want to wake up with a horse's head on my pillow.

What a cast of characters. There's Danny Bowes, the gimlet-eyed strategist; Luke Morley, the thinker, who laughs exactly like Chris Tarrant; Ben Matthews, the forthright comedian, and a man of courage; Chris Childs, the sensible one (all bass players are); and Harry James, the butt of most of the intra-band piss-taking, and also the man most built to take it (and give it back).

It kills me how the stories in this book vary slightly from member to member. That's what 30 years of drinking and falling over does for you. The tone of this book is generally irreverent, as you'd expect from this bunch of south-east London chancers, but then again there's been no fluffing of the facts and absolutely no lying. Despite the band members' love of a jape and a quip, they've been through tribulations that would leave any other band weeping in the corner, and when those moments come, they address them head-on. Thunder are all about self-belief and facing the enemy down. As Danny says when you ask him what the name of their record label, STC, stands for: "It's Straight Talk Company. I give you the news the same way; whether it's good or bad, I give it to you straight."

So it's hats off to Danny, Luke, Ben, Chris, Harry, Andy Taylor, Mark 'Snake' Luckhurst, Mikael 'Micke' Höglund, Nick Linden, Malcolm McKenzie, Mark Harris, Martin Burke, Roger Searle, Rod Smallwood, Ross Halfin and Mick Wall for their time and patience when it came to digging deep into the old memory banks for scurrilous tales about Thunder's past. Thanks to Lisa Bardsley for coming up with the idea of a Thunder book, David Barraclough for asking me to write it, and Matt Coulson at Thunder HQ for the cups of tea.

I think you're going to enjoy this book. I certainly loved writing it. I might put all the unforgivably rude stories in another book in a few years, unless Danny pays me a lot of money not to.

Joel McIver, 2016

THE GUILTY PARTIES

IT'S ALL THEIR FAULT...

MEMBERS OF THUNDER

DANNY BOWES, VOCALS

LUKE MORLEY, GUITAR

BEN MATTHEWS, GUITAR AND KEYBOARDS

CHRIS CHILDS, BASS

GARY 'HARRY' JAMES, DRUMS

FORMER MEMBERS OF THUNDER

MARK 'SNAKE' LUCKHURST, BASS, 1989 – 1992

MIKAEL 'MICKE' HÖGLUND, BASS, 1993 – 1995

PROLOGUE: DONINGTON AUGUST 18 1990

Danny Bowes So there we were, in front of 80,000 people, at the biggest rock and metal festival on the planet. My voice was fucked. I hadn't been able to speak, let alone sing, for five days. If I couldn't sing these songs, everything we'd worked for would be wasted. No pressure, then...

Luke Morley I was terrified. It was the size of the crowd that got me. How do you play with 80,000 people watching you?

Mark 'Snake' Luckhurst I was crapping myself. I thought we were going to get buckets of piss thrown at us. And Danny literally couldn't speak. He would open his mouth and nothing would come out.

Harry James That was squeaky-bum time. I had serious stage fright. I wasn't sure how this massive gig was going to pan out for us.

Ben Matthews We were terrified that Danny wouldn't be able to sing. I still remember, half an hour before stage time, that there was a stony silence in our dressing room.

Harry The first note that came out of Danny's mouth was fantastic. I still remember the relief and elation I felt at that moment.

Ben If you find the footage online, you can actually see the moment when we realised that the gig was going to be good: it's when Danny hits a high note in the middle of the first song, 'She's So Fine'. Before that, I dropped my plectrum three times, I was so nervous. Once we knew that Danny's voice was OK, we nailed that gig. We looked good, we sounded good and we knew we were good.

Danny So how the fuck did a bunch of idiots from south-east London get to this point?

Left: Luke demonstrating his artistic temperament with a Magic Marker.

1960–1974

IN WHICH OUR HEROES ARE BORN, GROW UP, ARE SEDUCED BY THE POWER OF ROCK MUSIC AND MANAGE TO GET THROUGH SCHOOL MOSTLY UNSCATHED, ALTHOUGH DANNY DOES GET INJURED QUITE A LOT.

Danny Bowes I was born in West Ham in London on April 14, 1960. My mum was a typical East End earth mother: very loving. My father was 19 when I was born, with no money or prospects, and consequently very angry and resentful. When my dad wasn't working, he was either in the pub playing darts or out fishing. He loved the outdoors: he should have been a park ranger, really. Even though he was rarely at home, I grew up completely terrified of him: I had to count down from 10 in my head before I could speak to him. When I got to zero I would blurt out, "Dad", and he'd say, "Yes?" Sometimes I'd lose confidence at that point and walk away. Then I'd curse myself for being afraid.

Luke Morley I was born in St Giles' Hospital in Camberwell on June 19, 1960. My upbringing was quite messy at first. My parents were both very young. They were both art teachers, but they'd been students when they met. My father, who was originally from Derbyshire, was at Goldsmiths College when I was born and he went on to the Royal College of Art, which meant he was lucky enough to avoid National Service. My mum went to Camberwell Art School and had been brought up in a large family in London.

When I popped into the world, they were living with my maternal grandmother.

Harry James I was born in Stone Park Hospital in Beckenham, Kent, on December 14, 1960, close to Crystal Palace's football ground. I'm a major CPFC fan. It was our local club, after all. I had a very stable family background; my father was the local butcher in Penge. My mother worked at the local printers. I have a sister, who is lovely and far more intelligent than I'll ever be. Thankfully, she also has more hair.

Ben Matthews I was born at home on July 21, 1963, on the border between Blackheath and Lewisham. My mother said I was very convenient, which I've always

teased her about. She told me, "I had breakfast, I had you, and then I had lunch."
I've got two older brothers and a younger sister. You hear about competition in a band: well, there's a lot of competition in my family, mainly for food. We used to try and steal each other's potatoes, and I usually ended up being stabbed in the hand with a fork... But we were very close, and we still are. I had a truly idyllic childhood. I'm the luckiest person on this planet, there's no doubt about it. Great parents, good schools. I was at John Ball Primary School in Blackheath – it's still there. My father was an architect and always busy, but always around too. My mother was a teacher. We had holidays in France and were incredibly middle class.

Chris Childs I was born at home in Writtle, Essex on June 24, 1959 to a working-class family. My father was a carpenter and a builder: anything that could be fabricated, he could turn his hand to. My mother was head cook at the local school. My brother, a few years older than me, was the singer in a local band, and I was constantly in awe of what he did. The die was cast at a very early age – there was never a doubt in my mind as to how I would be spending the rest of my life.

Above: Luke with his grandfather on Brighton beach.
Right: Danny the bashful one (top left), Ben the gardener (top right), Harry wearing his new high-waisted beach pants (below right) and Chris struggling to close a deckchair (below left).

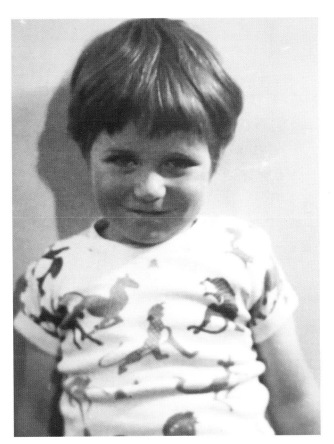

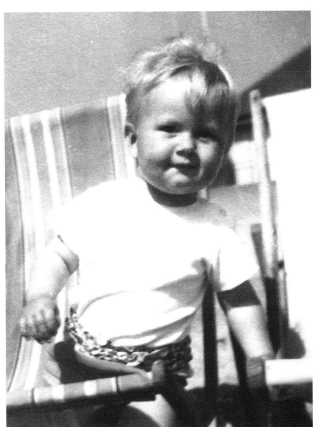

Danny I grew up very bookish. My dad taught me to read when I was very young. I used to spend a lot of time thinking, and wondering why things were the way they were. I always wanted to know why things happened: I was constantly evaluating and analysing. I also used to add up the number of letters in every word I read. I did that for years. First I added up all the letters in a line, then in a page, and then in a chapter, and I kept a running total in my head of how many letters there were in each. I don't know why I did it, but I didn't question it either. To me it felt normal. Part of my brain was doing that all the time, while I was digesting the story.

It was only revealed when I was 14 years old and the English teacher at school asked if any of us had any unusual habits while reading. I think he probably meant with bookmarks or turning the corners of pages over, and so on. I put my hand up and told him what I did. He said, "I don't believe you. Come back tomorrow and I'll test you." So I went back the next day and he tested me. He couldn't believe it, but instead of congratulating me like I thought he would, he told me I was weird. I was shocked, and it destroyed me, and I stopped doing it there and then. I can't do it any more, but I'm handy to have around when others are doing crosswords, as I can still recall the number of letters in a lot of words. I know, the teacher was probably right – I'm weird.

> I CAN STILL REMEMBER THE TWISTED GLEE IN HIS EYES AS HE WATCHED ME FAIL TO MAKE THE TURN, SHOOT OFF THE PAVEMENT AND HEAD STRAIGHT INTO THE TRAFFIC, UNDER THE 122 BUS.

Above: Danny, pictured between escapades.
Opposite top row: Danny with his sister Susie, Aunt Irene and Uncle George; Luke (pictured at front left) delivering food to the elderly at Buxton Harvest Festival; and Chris as a cowboy...
Opposite middle row: ...and a spaceman, alongside Ben wondering why he had to wear that jumper.
Bottom row: Harry learning to party hard at an early age.

Luke When I was two and a half we moved to Scarborough, and my parents both got jobs at the art college there. It was at that point it all started going wrong! They split up shortly after that and moved to Newcastle for a while, before separating. My mum moved back down to live with her parents and my father moved to Bournemouth. It was all reasonably amicable, but in the interim I was a bit pillar to post. I went to primary school in Brighton, Bournemouth and Buxton.

Danny I was injured a lot as a kid. First, when I was three years old, I ran after a football when it rolled into the road and a car hit me. I was dragged along for several yards with the front bumper lodged in my lip. I had stitches in my mouth, head and lip and I still have the scars today, as well as no feeling in the left side of my mouth. Two years after that I somehow ended up in the deep end of a swimming pool and had to have the water pumped out of my lungs by the lifeguard.

At the age of six, the kid next door removed the brakes from my tricycle, telling me that this would turn it into a 'drag bike'. We decided that the best way to test my new mean machine would be for me to ride from the top of the hill down to the bottom, turning the corner as quickly as possible. I can still remember the twisted glee in his

eyes as he watched me fail to make the turn, shoot off the pavement and head straight into the traffic, under the 122 bus.

Luckily for me, the driver managed to brake quickly. My bike was destroyed, and I was bruised and shocked, but that wasn't the end of it. Two old ladies dragged me out, marched me home, and proceeded to scold my mother for not exercising control over her son. This resulted in an early night and the obligatory clip round the ear from first my mum and then my dad when he got home. Talk about a bad day. Funnily enough, I never played with that boy again.

Chris My parents were always incredibly supportive of my interest in music. They bought me my first acoustic guitar from Traffords catalogue, with the promise that if I could learn to play that, I could have an electric one – which I did, and they kept to their word. My father converted an old gramophone for me to use as an amplifier until my brother gave me my first real amp. My dad would take days off work to take my gear to gigs. I've no idea how their house is still standing, with the amount of gear I used to squeeze into my bedroom.

Luke Music was massively important in my family. I remember the excitement in the house when The Beatles released *A Hard Day's Night* in 1964. My parents weren't musical themselves, but when my father was young he had an uncle who offered to pay for him to learn a musical instrument. He didn't take up his uncle's offer, and he always regretted it. I don't remember this, but I was given a toy electric guitar and I'd stand in the corner and play it. I was a bit shy, so apparently I'd stand with my back to the room.

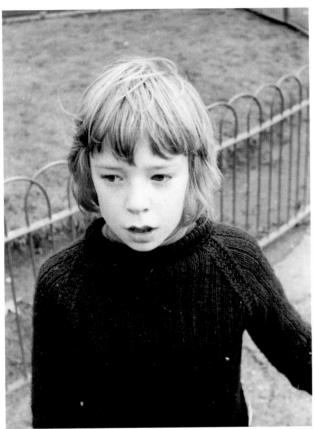

Danny When I was five, we moved from the flat above a betting office in Plaistow in East London to Plumstead, south of the river. The new place was another flat above a shop, but this one was my grandad's. He was like Sid James: a complete rogue, but very entertaining. He could walk into a pub full of strangers and leave there several hours later, very pissed, and friends with everyone. My dad told me a story about a car ride with my grandad and his four siblings. My grandad parked in a pub car park, went in, came back three minutes later with bags of crisps for them, then went back in. Ninety minutes later he came back to the car and made them all get out and walk home. Turns out he'd sold the car to someone in the pub. Nutter! I loved him. My dad didn't get on with him when he was a kid, and from what I was told it seems there was quite a lot of action with a belt. We had no money; it took years and years before that changed.

Luke When I was seven years old it was agreed that I would go and live with my father's parents in Buxton in Derbyshire, which is why I'm a Manchester City supporter. I lived there until 1969. It was a lovely place to live.

Danny We moved to Eltham in 1967, which was a much nicer place. We had a typical council house with a big green outside and a bunch of kids playing on it. That year, my mother made me go and get a haircut from a local pensioner, because it was cheap. It turned out he was blind. Literally blind. I was completely bald when I came out of there. At that age, you can imagine the ridicule. After that, whenever my mum told me I had to get a haircut, I would run away from home and not come back until it was dark. By the age of 11, I had hair down to my arse. I looked feral, and I pretty much was feral. I used to climb trees a lot, and I got run over nine times – mostly by cars, and once by a motorbike. I

was always hurting myself in various ways, regularly came home covered in blood, and I must have been a constant worry to my parents.

Luke By 1969 mum had set herself up in London, so I moved back there. My parents are friends to this day, which is good. My dad remarried and had two kids, so I have a half-brother and a half-

sister on his side. My mother settled down again and my sister came along. So there are two family groups, if you like.

Harry Something obviously went wrong somewhere: I was an intelligent kid, and went to grammar school and got loads of O levels, but it all went downhill as soon as I discovered rock music. I loved Deep Purple: Ian Paice was pretty much number one on my list of drummers. The first band I ever saw play live was Budgie, and they were absolutely brilliant.

I got interested in drums when I was eight or nine. I used to play drums on my parents' chairs at home, and managed to ruin them completely. I used to tap them with chopsticks and use a shoebox as a bass drum. The poor neighbours were heading for a nervous breakdown, so my mum and

dad eventually decided to get me a practice drum kit. That was a bit later, in 1972.

Luke To this day, I'm obsessed with the chronology of The Beatles: I'll bore anyone rigid with them. There were always tons of Beatles, Stones and Dylan LPs around the house. I remember going down to my dad's place in Bournemouth and going through his records, and I found the first Jimi Hendrix album, a classic Chuck Berry LP and a Cream compilation. I played those albums relentlessly, and realised at that point that cool music was all about the guitar.

I was 10 when I started playing it myself. My father's second wife Linda had a Spanish guitar lying around, so I had a go on it, as all kids do. I started off playing right-handed, but as soon as I got into Hendrix I flipped it over. I harangued my father until he bought me a Spanish acoustic guitar for my eleventh birthday; it was right-handed, but I changed the strings over. I learned by ear initially.

At the same time, my best friend in primary school in Deptford, Tony Myers, got a guitar from his uncle, who smoked Embassy cigarettes and bought him the guitar with the cigarette tokens. We were both obsessed with T. Rex and learned how to play guitar together. Later, Tony and I stayed good mates even though we went to separate schools. Between the ages of 11 and 18 we were constantly in each other's houses, playing the guitar. We're still good mates now.

Ben My mother played the piano, and she was very good. I started piano lessons when I was nine with the local vicar's wife at the vicarage. I can play by ear, which is both an advantage and a disadvantage: you can hear a piece of music and then play it, but it meant I didn't need to read the music. I never got as proficient at reading music as I could have, something I regret now. I started learning the guitar around the same time. I saw a band named Flintlock on TV, and I thought, "I'd really like to do that." I looked at the instruments and thought, "I don't want to be a drummer: they're always at the back" – although Flintlock's drummer was actually the singer and sat at the front. I never considered being the singer, although I can hold a line of backing vocals. The guitarist played a gold-top Gibson Les Paul, but that looked far too complicated, so I thought I'd play bass instead. Fortunately my mum bought me a nylon-string acoustic guitar, and I ended up learning by playing along with records, piecing a song together like a jigsaw, solos and everything. I thoroughly enjoyed it.

Luke I went to see T. Rex at the Lewisham Odeon in 1971: my mother gave me two tickets for my eleventh birthday present. That gig had a massive impact on me. The palpable sense of excitement in the audience was what hit me hardest – the joy they were feeling was obvious. I'd only experienced that at football matches before. Afterwards, I went straight home on the bus and told my mum I wanted to play music for a living. She probably thought, "Oh shit."

My mother's mother was a very accomplished violinist. As a teenager she was offered a job in one of the big touring dance bands of the time, but her father wouldn't let her take it as the family was poor and needed the income from her job. After my grandfather died, she moved in with us for a little while, when I was about 15. She bought me my first expensive guitar, a Fender Stratocaster. That was lovely of her. Later, she came to see Thunder play at the Hammersmith Odeon, which was great.

Danny I was obsessed with music. I remember I once walked five miles to a record shop to buy David Bowie's *Aladdin Sane* LP. It cost £2.39, and I only had £2.29. The shop assistant sent me away. I walked all the way home to get the extra 10p, and then I walked back to the shop to get the record, then I walked home again. I walked 20 miles just to get that album.

Ben When I was a kid, my elder brothers – one of whom is now into opera and will deny ever being into rock music – had control of the family record player. They were into Led Zep, The Who, the Stones, Deep Purple and similar bands. As a result, my musical taste was relatively advanced: at the age of nine I was listening to music that 14-year-olds were into, a lifetime's difference at that age. To put it in perspective, my mates at school were listening to The Wombles.

Harry My parents were huge fans of rock music. I remember my dad going nuts when the guitar solo started in Lynyrd Skynyrd's 'Freebird'. He always wanted to play

music himself, but never got the chance. His family business, a butcher's shop, had started in 1903, but he discouraged me from following on in the business. He said, "It's too bloody cold in the winter and too bloody hot in the summer. I'd prefer you to follow your dream, son."

Danny My junior school was a place called Ealdham Square in Eltham – it's still there, nestled in a massive council estate. All life was there. In my final year, my teacher recognised that I was bright and told my parents, "This boy needs to go to a grammar school." They were completely chuffed. I wanted to go to the local comprehensive where my mates were going, but no, I had to go to Haberdashers' Aske's, which was in New Cross. That was like going to Scotland for me. I had to get two buses or a train and walk five miles, and I didn't want to do that, but they said I had to go. And of course, for my mum, that meant I had to get my hair cut. I made my usual bolt for the door but my dad was ready and barred the way. I'll never forget his words: "You need to get a haircut, or your mother will get upset, and if that happens, I will hurt you." I accepted I couldn't win, went to the barbers and got a short back and blowlamp. I was choked.

> **AT THE AGE OF NINE I WAS LISTENING TO MUSIC THAT 14-YEAR-OLDS WERE INTO, A LIFETIME'S DIFFERENCE AT THAT AGE. TO PUT IT IN PERSPECTIVE, MY MATES AT SCHOOL WERE LISTENING TO THE WOMBLES.**

Left: Luke with his sister Nina.
Above: David Bowie's 1973 LP *Aladdin Sane*. After walking 20 miles to get it, Danny accidentally melted his copy by leaving it against a chimney breast.

Luke I started at Haberdashers' Aske's in September 1971. It was very strange to me, coming from a primary school in Deptford, to see them all walking around in gowns and so on. I'd never been around affluent people like that before. It was the best school in the area, though, and quite socially aspirational, which I found odd, because my mother was an avid socialist and it was slightly against her principles to send me there. However, my primary school headmistress had written to my mum, saying, "We think Luke should go to Aske's," and she wanted me to get the best education, so I was packed off there.

Danny When I got to Aske's for the interview, the place was like *Tom Brown's Schooldays*. Masters and prefects gliding around in gowns and wearing mortarboards everywhere. As I waited for my turn, directly opposite me I saw a kid with the biggest head I'd ever seen, and huge amounts of bright red hair. It was Luke, with his mum.

Luke Danny remembers me because my hair was ridiculously long and he'd been through the trauma of having his hair cut. When he saw me, he was fuming, but his mum said, "Don't worry dear, that boy won't get in."

Danny I said to her, "If he does, I'll never speak to you again!"

Luke I did pass the interview, but I found out on my first day that they didn't play football at Aske's, which really pissed me off. That was a shattering blow for me at that age. And I had to cut my hair after all, after being told off about it five times on the first day. You had to wear a cap in the first year, which was a real source of misery for me.

> I HATED ASKE'S FROM THE MOMENT I ARRIVED UNTIL I LEFT FIVE YEARS LATER. IT WAS TOO STRICT, WITH TOO MUCH DISCIPLINE, AND I DIDN'T LIKE WEARING THE UNIFORM AND A CAP.

It was very different to what I was used to: on the day we arrived, I met the Head of Lower School, who was a terrifying man with a handlebar moustache and a finger missing from the war. He used to bang the stump on tables to make his point.

Danny I hated Aske's from the moment I arrived until I left five years later. It was too strict, with too much discipline, and I didn't like wearing the uniform and a cap. I never stopped hating it, although years later I realised the value of having been there.

Luke I was aware of Danny as soon as I got to Aske's: he was very funny. We had to improvise in drama and he was very good at that. He was from Eltham, and a whole gang of kids came from there and used to go home on the bus together.

Danny I have two brothers, Andrew and Michael, and a sister, Susie. Michael became very ill when I was 12 or 13. He had influenza and double pneumonia at the same time, and was minutes from death. He spent months in hospital, and mistakes were made with his treatment. It was an awful time for my parents: my dad had to work because we didn't have any money, and my mum spent the whole time camped out at the hospital.

Consequently, the remaining three of us were palmed off to relatives; I went to stay with my

Auntie Carol, my dad's sister. She was married with two sons and lived in Suffolk. She was only about eight years older than me, so I massively identified with her. She was also a bit of a rebel, so I thought she was very cool. And she had records – piles of them. I was a kid from Eltham in the middle of the Suffolk countryside and I had no idea what to do with myself, so I sat there and worked my way through them; it took weeks to listen to them all. She had really eclectic tastes: everything was in there. Jethro Tull, Sam Cooke, Deep Purple, The Beatles... it really affected me. She had a monogram, which was a record player with a lift-up lid, and she said she was going to buy a stereogram (luxury), so I begged her to give me the monogram. Months later it magically appeared at our house. I didn't know how it got there, but I was extremely chuffed.

Ben I wasn't able to go to my first choice of secondary school. The option they gave me was a very rough comprehensive school – nowhere near Aske's, I hasten to add. My mother was having none of it, so she decided to home school me. It was great fun: I didn't start lessons until 11 a.m., with coffee and toast. She covered just about every subject, but eventually they found a place for me at Thomas Tallis, a brand new school. It was very well equipped and had a very modern attitude towards teaching. Boys learned to cook and girls played rugby – this was back in 1974, remember.

Harry I got my first drum kit in 1972 and a week later I was playing social clubs. I advanced quite quickly on the drums, playing in a club band which I think was called Silva Jade. Another was Fojomocog, which was the initials of all the

Above: The coat of arms of Haberdasher's Askes Hatcham Boys Grammar School, as attended by Danny and Luke.

members; I was the G at the end, because my real first name is Gary. We all wore white trousers and different-coloured satin shirts. It was absolutely ridiculous, but it worked at the time. We did pubs and clubs and earned good money. I think it was a pretty good grounding and start to my career. I became the drummer I am today because I went out and played gigs, rather than practising on my own in a rehearsal room.

Chris During my teenage years my schooldays were spent planning my next gig in the school hall, and clambering around over the stage focusing lights. All my time at home was devoted to recording, learning songs or building speaker cabinets. I played six-string guitar from the age of 12 until I was 16, always fronting my own bands as lead guitarist and singer, totally obsessed with Ritchie Blackmore. I once mercilessly fired the rhythm guitarist for playing louder than me at a rehearsal! Fortunately I saw the light and changed to bass, learning all I could from records in as many different styles as possible.

Malcolm McKenzie In the first half-term of 1973, I moved from my old school to Aske's. Danny, Luke and I were all in the same class together.

Danny I had a fight with Malcolm the first day we were at school together. I can't remember what it was about. He pinned me down and said, "Do you give up?" and I said yes, but the moment he let go I hit him again.

Malcolm At the time Luke was very short; he had a growth spurt later on. He was a quiet lad with a big mop of ginger hair who would sit at the back of the class. I'd met him before when I played rugby against him, a few months before I joined their school. He had quite a sarcastic sense of humour, and he had a group of mates who I didn't really know.

Danny was one of the popular kids:

everybody liked him. He was much easier to get to know, but much harder to get to know well, if that makes sense. In fact, they're both quite difficult to get to know well, but after 40 years you get the idea. In

the spring, we went on a school trip to Scotland and did a lot of hiking. I got chatting to Luke on one hike and we discovered that we both liked rock music. All that day we chatted about stuff, which is how we became friends.

Danny In 1974 we moved again, this time to the other end of Eltham, to a much nicer place. By then my dad had made some money; we had new furniture and new carpets and a new colour telly. Before that, everything had been second-hand. I was working for my dad on Saturday mornings, paying off a skiing trip that I wanted to go on.

He did me the best favour. I told him the trip was going to cost £70 and he said,

"That's a lot of money. If you work for me every Saturday between now and the trip, I'll pay for it." I worked for him for three hours every Saturday after that, but I never went on the trip – I have no idea why. But I liked working with him, because I saw a side of him that I'd not seen before, and our relationship changed quite a bit. I liked the banter with the customers and the other guys in the shop, and I had a sense of purpose. I enjoyed it much more than going to school. After I left school later on, I went to work for him in the carpet warehouse. Once I'd passed my test, I was soon driving a van and fitting carpets, but mostly so I had the use of the van after work, so we could do gigs.

Luke In 1974 my dad took a job at Manchester Polytechnic and I'd go and see him up there. The net effect of all the moving around when I was a kid was that I learned to make friends quite quickly. I don't think my parents' separation had any serious effect on me. They've always been gregarious, sociable types and I was generally a happy kid.

Danny I got mugged in 1974. There was a comprehensive school near Aske's. It was rough, and those kids used to nick our money on the way to school. It happened to me, and I gave everything to them because I had no confidence. That soon changed.

That was also the year I went to my first live show. It was Bad Company at the Rainbow Theatre in London. The tickets were £2.20 each, including the booking fee, and I went with my mate Jon. They opened with 'Deal With The Preacher', from their unreleased second album. Only the band knew the song. I bought a huge poster, which got crushed in the tube door on the way home. When I opened it up they had no heads, but I put it on the wall anyway. It changed my life. The gig, I mean, not the poster.

Above: Harry knocks 'em dead in a holiday talent contest. Look at those flowing locks...

1975—1981

THREE BANDS FIGHT FOR SUPREMACY IN BLACKHEATH IN SOUTH-EAST LONDON: NUTHIN' FANCY, WHITE NOIZE AND MOON TIER. DESPITE THEIR TERRIBLE FASHION SENSE, OUR MEN CUT THEIR TEETH IN FINE STYLE. FAME BECKONS!

Luke In the first two years at Aske's, my grades were pretty good – all As, Bs and Cs. The following year it all went wrong, when my friend Tony Myers introduced me to a drummer called Paul Caple. Paul had just got his first drum kit, and I spent every waking hour for the next few months making a dreadful racket in his mum's attic, which doubled as his bedroom. Then we found a bass player, Gary Condon, a mate of Paul's. Tony Myers would come and play bass sometimes, but it was all a bit of a mess, to be honest. Malcolm McKenzie, who later became Thunder's manager, was the singer.

Danny I'd never sung in a band, or even in the school choir. I'd only sung along with records at home. I loved music, but I had no pretensions towards making it myself. It was only when I went over to Luke's house in December 1975 and saw Paul Caple's drum kit that I decided to sing. It was a bright red Pearl Maxwin Vistalite kit, and to me it looked incredible. I couldn't believe how shiny the chrome was: it was as if sparks were coming off it. I spent all day thinking about it, and all that night trying to work out how I could be near one. I didn't have any money, though, and I couldn't play any instrument, so I had no choice: I had to be a singer.

Luke The next day, Danny sat down next to me in economics and said, "I hear you've got a band." He told me he was a singer and that he had a microphone, which made me think he must be good. We had the temerity to make him audition over at Paul's house, which he did – and it turned out that he could really sing.

Danny I thought I sounded dreadful, and I couldn't believe how hard it was to sing while performing, compared to singing along in the bathroom at home. By the end of the afternoon, I couldn't speak.

Luke His voice was pretty much all there, even back then. He didn't sound much different then to how he did later.

Danny They made me go and make the tea while they talked about me, and when I came back, they said, "You're in." So it was Luke's job to tell Malcolm that he was no longer the singer, but he kept putting it off, so after two weeks I said, "Either you tell Malcolm, or I will." I wanted my moment.

Malcolm I couldn't sing a note, although I could play a bit

> **I THOUGHT I SOUNDED DREADFUL, AND I COULDN'T BELIEVE HOW HARD IT WAS TO SING WHILE PERFORMING, COMPARED TO SINGING ALONG IN THE BATHROOM AT HOME. BY THE END OF THE AFTERNOON, I COULDN'T SPEAK.**

of guitar, so when Luke heard Danny's singing, I was told in no uncertain terms that I couldn't be the singer but I could be the bass player. It was quite tactfully done, actually. I saved up, bought a bass and an amp – but I was rubbish at bass too.

Luke Gary dropped out and Danny became the singer, so Malcolm switched to bass.

Danny I think Malcolm was probably OK with me becoming the singer when he switched to bass. Our relationship was always edgy, so it was hard to tell really.

Luke We'd play anything we could physically manage to do: a couple of Hendrix songs, a couple of Dr Feelgood songs. We progressed to a few Lynyrd Skynyrd numbers and maybe a bit of Thin Lizzy too. We called ourselves Kamikaze for about five minutes, until Danny came up with the name Nuthin' Fancy, after the Lynyrd Skynyrd LP. The first gig we did was at my old primary school. We took the drums to the school on the bus, after two bus conductors refused to take us. We just threw the drums on the third bus and ignored the conductor.

Right Lynyrd Skynyrd's third studio album, *Nuthin' Fancy* from 1975, provided the name for Danny and Luke's fledgling band.

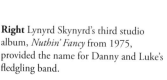

Danny Our second gig was supposed to be in our school's biology department, and we got paid £16 for it. We were supporting the local heroes: another school band called Vena Cava. They had their own PA, which we borrowed. I was elected as the man who had to go and talk about the arrangements with the teacher. I must have known that I was the manager type even back then: we were going to get a pound more than Vena Cava did! But we never actually got to do the gig, because a labourer down the road put a pickaxe through a power line in the ground, cutting off the school's electricity and killing himself in the process. I thought that was very inconsiderate of him.

Luke I liked doing gigs. I'm not the biggest show-off in the world, but I do love playing guitar, and being onstage gives me an excuse to jump around like an idiot.

Danny When I went onstage and sang with the band, it was a huge rush, and it was great to get applause, but initially I found it hard to look at the audience, so I spent a lot of the time with my back to them. I must have looked like I was singing to the drummer. Luke said, "Mate, if we're going to get famous, the audience needs to see you singing the songs." I knew he was right, but – believe it or not – I found it very hard to face them. I was convinced they could hear all the bum notes I was singing. It took me a long time to become the megalomaniac I am today. We played 'Jumpin' Jack Flash' and 'Brown Sugar' by The Rolling Stones, songs by ZZ Top, Dr Feelgood, Free, Bad Company, Thin Lizzy, Led Zeppelin, Jimi Hendrix... any band around whose songs we could physically reproduce.

Luke When Nuthin' Fancy started rehearsing at my mother's house, the volume of it was immense. There were complaints from the neighbours, but she always encouraged me to make music.

Danny Were we a good band? No, we were bloody terrible, but we thought we were great, and that's half the battle. We got better with each gig, and our confidence grew.

Chris In 1975 my Uncle Ken, who sang regularly in pubs, got an audition for *Opportunity Knocks*. He asked my band to back him, and off we went to the TV studios in Norwich, under the name of Mr Publand & His Nephews. Ken wanted to sing the Tom Jones version of 'Delilah' – we played the Alex Harvey version. Hughie Green looked like he was going to cry, but at least he let us finish the song.

Luke I met a chap called Martin Burke when he gave my mum a lift home in 1975. He taught an evening class in photography at the same college where my mum taught drawing. He really influenced the music we listened to as teenagers, because his mate worked at *Melody Maker* and gave Martin all sorts of American albums by artists like Nils Lofgren, Springsteen and Boston before anyone over here had heard them.

Martin Burke Christine, Luke's mum, was teaching a life drawing class at the Eltham Institute, where I taught photography. One night, she asked me if I could give Luke some tips on the guitar, so I asked him to show me his guitar playing. My mouth dropped open because he was so good, even at the age of 15. He ended up giving *me*

advice about guitar playing. He was a keen, intelligent kid, quite sporty, and devoted to his guitar above all else.

Luke Martin was Nuthin' Fancy's first manager, and he also played guitar in a local group called the Brockley Boogie Band. I used to hang out at Martin's house whenever his band were rehearsing. As a result I ended up playing with them whenever someone in the band didn't show up. I played drums (not very well), bass, guitar, sang backing vocals or whatever was needed. Danny and I both roadied for them at various points. Martin always very kindly paid me in beer!

Martin I remember that Nuthin' Fancy had a gig in a basement cellar bar, for which they weren't going to be paid, so I went and saw the manager and persuaded him to give them five quid, although he didn't want to pay them anything. They were delighted! Then I managed them for a while, getting them gigs and trying to get them a record deal.

Luke Insanely, our parents let Danny, me and our schoolmate Jon go to the Reading Festival in the summer of 1975. We camped there and it was great: the bill was fantastically eclectic, when you think about it. The headliners were Yes, Hawkwind and Wishbone Ash, and in the daytime you had Joan Armatrading, Judas Priest, Thin Lizzy, UFO, Mahavishnu Orchestra, Kursaal Flyers, Supertramp... it was one of those weekends you never forget. John Peel was there, and it was also the first time I heard a record by Steely Dan. Of course, it all went slightly wrong when I kicked over the camping stove and the boiling water went all over Danny's ankle and he had to go to hospital. He got it all bandaged up and came back. To this day he'll tell you how clumsy I am.

Above: Reading Festival, 1975. Danny and Luke are there, aged 15. What were their parents thinking?

Danny I had terrible hay fever as a teenager, and by the time O levels came round in 1976 it just destroyed me. I just could not concentrate – I felt like I'd been run over by a truck. My mother gave me a bottle of Benylin cough syrup and said, "Use this." A spoonful of that would make the hay fever go away, but after a while I started to need more and more. It's probably not the same now, but in those days, if you drank a bottle of Benylin, it made you very aggressive. They gave it to all the players in the school rugby team before they played, to get them all fucked up. So I changed, over the course of that summer, from a shy kid who lacked confidence and who always had his head in a book, adding up letters in words, to someone who wanted to kill people. I didn't know it was to do with the Benylin: I thought I was just an angry young man.

On the way to school, the same kids who had mugged me the year before tried to do it again. Let's just say it got very physical, and I didn't lose any pens. I went to school with a black eye, looking like I'd been run over. There were several incidents, including one with the school bully: a great big kid who was, shall we say, not very academic. He accused me of sitting in his chair in maths, even though the teacher had put me in that seat because of the seating system he used.

The big guy's name was Chris, and he told me I was going to get my head kicked in at lunchtime. I was shitting myself, but when he started on me I just snapped, and jumped on him. He fell over, mostly because he was surprised, and I was winning for about 15 seconds; then he recovered from the shock and started pummelling me. Luckily the teacher came in and broke it up before he did me too much damage, but by then it was too late for him – I was a hero.

So now I had a reputation as a scrapper, which was a load of bollocks really, because I wasn't a fighter at all. I had boxed for a little while up until I was about 14, so I

knew how to punch and take one too, but I think being in the band was what really changed me. My confidence grew and grew as we got better, and the audiences got louder and louder. One fed the other. I might have become more confident anyway, I don't know, but the band definitely served a very useful purpose.

Luke I had a job at Bejam for six weeks in the hot summer of 1976, loading boxes of frozen turkeys. Jesus, those things are heavy.

Shortly after that I got a Saturday job at Boots, which was great because the money was good. I worked there full-time the following summer, mopping up the odd spilled bottle of Brut and so on. Every Saturday, without fail, some tosser would break one. To this day the smell of Brut and Old Spice makes me feel sick.

Danny I did quite well in my English and history O levels, came close to passing in geography and economics, and failed maths, because I didn't see why trigonometry and sines and cosines – which I basically thought of as witchcraft – were relevant to me. So I left school and spent that hot summer of 1976 working for my dad, skinny-dipping late at night in my local open-air pool, and playing with a lovely girl called Lorraine.

Luke I didn't get good O level results: I think I got four, enough to scrape into the sixth form. I wanted to leave school, but my mum insisted that I stay on and do A

levels. I failed them all miserably, although while bunking off lessons I did manage to perfect my smoking technique. I think mum was probably disappointed that I'd done so badly academically, but she didn't really let on. Once I was out of school, Tony Myers managed to get me a job in the warehouse at MFI in Catford, where he worked. It was hard, physical graft but there was an entertaining mixture of characters working there, and it allowed me to get enough money together to buy a nice guitar and amp, which was all I was really interested in at the time.

Ben I was lucky: I found exams quite easy and managed to get nine O levels, even taking a couple of them a year early. I stayed on into the sixth form and passed three science A levels. I hadn't taken physics O level, but persuaded the teacher that I could do the A level without it. He agreed and was so happy when I passed. I admit that I was a bit of a swot at school – it was the best reason to grow your hair and form a rock band, and stops any bullying. Now I was under a great deal of pressure from my school and, to an extent, from my parents, to go to university. I went through the application process and got a place to read chemistry. There was no chance of me going, though, because I wanted to be in a band, so I said I wanted a year off beforehand and promptly applied for a job at a record company.

Danny It was a good time: my hair was growing back, I was in a band, and things were going well, but I couldn't tell my dad I'd left school or he'd go mental. I had nothing to lose, so with a bit of coaching from Lorraine, I talked my way into the sixth form at her school, Crown Woods in Eltham. Because I'd come from Aske's, I think the headmaster saw me as a bit of a glittering prize, so I went there to do A levels. Funnily enough, I couldn't handle the lack of discipline and left in 1977, after six months. I convinced my dad to give me a job after that.

Above: Luke in 1977, with his lifelong obsession already in full flow.

BIGNITE at St.Germain's Hotel
NUTHIN' FANCY
friday dec.16. *plus!* **Brockley Boogie Band**

Luke Nuthin' Fancy's first pub gigs were in 1977. We played at a place called the St Germaines Hotel, near where Brockley runs into Forest Hill. They had a dodgy back room and a basement where bands could play and get paid a tenner. We knew some of the other bands: my mate Tony was in a band which eventually became Moon Tier. We also played at the Rock Garden, and after that, when we'd left school, as many pub gigs as possible. It was a real adventure, looking back. The experience we gained there was invaluable. Occasionally I'd have those dreams where you walk onstage and there's only one string on your guitar, and it's the one that's out of tune! I don't think I ever experienced stage fright until we played Donington in 1990, and I've never had it since.

Ben The first rock gig I saw was Be Bop Deluxe in 1977, when they recorded the *Live! In The Air Age* LP at Hammersmith Odeon. You can hear me deliberately whistling loudly between songs on that record. I'd made it onto my first LP! I also used to go to Lewisham Odeon and see bands as often as I could – I saw The Who, Thin Lizzy, Motörhead, Rush, Judas Priest and Status Quo and many more there. I saw Led Zeppelin at Knebworth too, and I saw Black Sabbath supported by Van Halen in 1978, which was the best thing I'd ever seen in my life. Van Halen blew me – and Black Sabbath – away.

Luke I saw Van Halen on that tour. It was completely eye-opening for me: no one had ever played the guitar like that before,

although it wasn't really applicable to the music I was playing because I'd gone so far down the Paul Kossoff and Eric Clapton route.

Lewisham Odeon was brilliant. I saw Deep Purple on the *Burn* tour there when I was 14. I saw Thin Lizzy there a few times, and Chuck Berry. I missed David Bowie when he played there on the *Aladdin Sane* tour. Then I started going a little further afield and saw Zeppelin at Earl's Court in 1975.

I remember the day Elvis died. The night before, Martin Burke had got free tickets to see Ted Nugent at Hammersmith, and it was the first time I ever went to a rock'n'roll aftershow party. It was in a Greek restaurant on Tottenham Court Road. We were all smashing plates. Then Ted Nugent walked in. I didn't speak to him – I was terrified.

Above: Danny, Luke and Martin Burke living the high life – fourth, fifth and sixth from left respectively.

Harry I left Ravensbourne Grammar School in Bromley in 1978, when I was 18. The drums had completely taken over my life by then, so I carried on playing with my club band and gaining lots of experience. Mum and dad had educated me into having a normal job to fall back on, so I got an apprenticeship at a travel agent. I was there for three years, still living at home. But I was getting more and more into the music, and there were lots of trips up to the St Moritz Club, followed by falling asleep on the night bus at three in the morning and getting off at the wrong stop. I was having the time of my life. How I managed it I don't know, but after the apprenticeship at the travel agent, I became the manager. My mind wasn't exactly on the job, though – bashing the drums was always at the forefront of my mind.

Ben I formed a band called White Noize at school. Nick Linden played bass and sang, Andy Taylor – not the guy from Duran Duran, or indeed Iron Maiden's management – was the other guitar player and sang, and Rob Grafton was the drummer. My parents, bless them, bought me a black Satellite Les Paul guitar for £69, which was a lot of money back then. It was only a basic little Gibson copy but it played brilliantly. It was a revelation to have an electric guitar. I only ever had one guitar lesson: it was at the Greenwich Young People's Theatre, which was a council-run arts place where you could turn up. I was a better guitar player than the teacher was.

Chris I got my first break at a local pub, the King's Arms in Chelmsford, where I regularly went to see a band called Prey. The bass player hadn't showed up, and the singer asked if there was a bassist in the house. Of course my hand shot up, and I subsequently joined the band, working three or four nights a week in pubs and clubs.

Luke Nuthin' Fancy's gigs were shocking. There'd be three people there, two of whom were pissed and didn't care, and the landlord would constantly be telling us to turn it down because the people in the next room were trying to eat their dinner. But we chanced upon one pub which was brilliant: the White Swan in Greenwich. It was a tiny little pub, with a little stage, but it was very popular with the bikers.

Ben The White Swan was run by Val and Alan. Val was a tasty-looking blonde and Al was a big fuck-off bloke with two of the most vicious dogs you've ever seen in your life. It was a brilliant pub. Al was so supportive of all the bands, not least because he made shedloads of money out of them playing there. We were down there either playing or watching other bands pretty much every weekend. It really was a thriving scene.

> ❝ THEY COULDN'T WINE AND DINE US, SO THEY HAD TO TIZER AND DINE US. WE EVENTUALLY CHOSE A MANAGER BASED ON HOW NICE HIS CAR WAS. AH, THE WISDOM OF YOUTH… ❞

Harry I joined a band called Moon Tier, which included Tony Myers on guitar; we got on very well. We played rock pubs and weren't a bad band, although we seemed to be hitting a brick wall after a while. Danny and Luke came along to see us play, which is how I first met them. We were friendly rivals with their band at the White Swan – it was us, Nuthin' Fancy and White Noize.

Chris Through a mutual friend I heard that a band called Hogg were looking for a bass player, so I contacted them and auditioned. After being offered the gig I rehearsed with them once, decided that they would probably never do much and quit. The guitarist was Nik Kershaw…

Ben White Noize were the stars of our school, despite the fact that I used to walk around in the sixth form with bare feet and an Afghan coat. We arranged all our shows off our own backs, which was pretty good for a bunch of 16-year-olds. We were a pretty decent little band, actually. We had three managers fighting to manage us, including Manfred Mann's manager Harry Maloney, even though we were just kids. They couldn't wine and dine us, so they had to Tizer and dine us. We eventually chose a manager based on how nice his car was. Ah, the wisdom of youth…

Nick Linden I played bass in White Noize with Ben, who I knew because we were at school doing A level maths together. He's a lovely guy – really funny. We played punk-influenced rock, I suppose, and any time one of the three bands would play at the White Swan, we'd go down and see them. There was a friendly rivalry, but it was healthy.

Three years before that, I'd played a show at the Marquee when I was 15, supporting Budgie, but when I turned up at the front door with my guitar I was refused entry – too young. They had no idea what to do, so I had to promise not to drink anything and they let me in.

Rock Band for pubs clubs parties – weddings discos

Nuthin' Fancy

ring Dan 850-7917 or Mac 852-2426

Right: A vintage Nuthin' Fancy poster – the only problem being that Danny didn't turn up for the photoshoot, thus the empty chair and trainers… (top) Chris's teenage band flaunting their equipment! (below right) Ben rehearsing with Andy Taylor (a different one) in White Noize. Note spanking white trousers (below left).

Luke Val and Al were great. We used to play there every other week. Moon Tier and White Noize were the other regular rock bands and we all got to know each other, going to the same parties and even going out with the same girls. It became a social group.

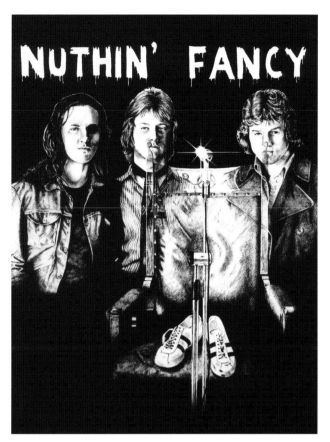

Luke Just before we started playing at the White Swan we had our first real personnel change. Chris Hussey was known locally as a great drummer. I remember he could play the drum break at the end of Zeppelin's 'Rock And Roll', which was very impressive. I remember telling Paul Caple we'd decided to ask Chris to join, and he was very reasonable about it.

Ben Moon Tier and Nuthin' Fancy were both really good bands, and they were our competition. We'd watch them and say to each other, "He can sing", "He's got a better guitar than me", "They've got more PA than we have... we need more PA!" Both bands had at least a couple of good songs.

We were always trying to outdo each other with pyrotechnics, even though we were playing in a pub. On many occasions you couldn't see the band for the smoke from the starbursts and the smoke bombs. Poor Nick was standing over a star burst when the idiot with his finger on the fire button set it off without looking. Nick looked up at me, slightly dazed and covered in black soot. This was health and safety, Seventies style.

Martin I was a freelance photographer, and when Luke left school and was looking for a job, he worked as my assistant for a while.

Luke It was really useful: I learned to process black-and-white film. Martin used to work for a label called Logo Records and we photographed The Tourists, which was Annie Lennox and Dave Stewart before they changed their name to Eurythmics. I remember I loaded the film into the camera backwards and Martin said, "Luke, you cunt!"

After I worked for Martin I managed to blag a job working in the Virgin Megastore, which was the first huge record shop in England. I worked in a stall in the middle of the shop selling concert tickets. I remember the day Abba tickets went on sale and there were queues halfway down Oxford Street. The funniest thing was the ticket touts who would try everything they could to butter you up. You could always spot them, as they all wore overcoats in summer and kept their hands in their pockets firmly on the cash.

Danny In 1979, the Tramshed in Woolwich put on a talent competition, and all three bands went in for it. We wanted the £100 prize money to make a demo. In those days recording was rare, and always an all-night affair. The results were invariably crap, as we had no idea what we were doing, but it was extremely exciting nonetheless.

Ben I want it in the book that White Noize beat Nuthin' Fancy in that talent competition!

Danny The reason White Noize won that competition was because they had a huge following of people who went to school with them, and their punters intimidated the judges. It's the truth! They said, "If you don't give the prize to White Noize, we'll kill you." We won our heat and then lost out on the last night. We were gutted.

Ben Max Splodge from Splodgenessabounds was a judge. I can't see a bunch of schoolkids intimidating a burly punk rocker... Perhaps we were just better looking or better at playing – or both, probably.

Danny The reason why that gig is so important to Thunder's history is that it was the first time we encountered a manager. His name was Robert Wace. He was very tall and looked like Christopher Lee: he wore a black cape, and was very posh.

Luke Robert was about six foot three and had a very plummy accent. He said, "I used to manage The Kinks. Would you describe yourselves as heavy metal?" and I said, "No, we're a rock band." He said, "Oh. It's a bit noisy in here. Can we talk in the gentlemen's toilets?" I was slightly concerned by this suggestion, although I needn't have worried. Just in case, though, Danny and our biggest roadie Derek – or Big D as he was more commonly known – came along to the gents too.

I'd never seen anyone quite like Robert before, but when he introduced himself, his name rang a bell, because my mum had been to art school with a guy called Barry Fantoni, who was a cartoonist for *Private Eye*. Barry knew Dave Davies of The Kinks, and I'd heard Barry telling my mum about some guy called Robert who was connected to that band.

Danny He said, "I think you're very good, and with my help you could be even better. Here's my card. Give me a call if you're interested." At that point, you could almost imagine him turning into a bat and flying out the window. We couldn't believe it – it was a really big deal for us.

Luke Robert obviously saw something in us, so I told Danny I thought we should go with him, and Danny agreed. At the same time, he and I felt that we were improving, but that Malcolm and Chris weren't. A guy had come up to me at the White Swan and said, "There are three average bands here – you could make one excellent one out of them if you wanted to," and a light went on over my head. So we called a meeting and told Malcolm and Chris they were fired. Chris told us he completely understood, but Malcolm didn't take it very well. It was the first difficult decision, in terms of music, that I'd made.

Malcolm Luke was always the best musician in Nuthin' Fancy, and Danny was an excellent singer, and I think they realised that they needed to move on without me if they were going to do anything remarkable – so I got the bullet. They figured that Nick Linden from White Noize would be better for the job of bassist, and they were right, but it was hurtful. I was told at a meeting at Luke's house, and we fell out for a few months over it, but then I went to see them play and they were a lot better than they'd been before. We became friends again as time passed.

Danny I've no idea what Robert saw in Nuthin' Fancy. He probably didn't make any money out of us, but he gave us some good advice. He told us to be nice to people on the way up, because you'll probably meet them again on the way down. He also introduced us to a great lawyer and accountant, and he told me never to let anyone sign the cheques. I never have.

Mind you, we took the piss out of Robert something rotten, because he was so odd. We used to drive over to his apartment in South Kensington in our old Bedford van that cost us 50 quid, and we'd take all our mates with us. He'd be putting golf balls in his front room, it was like an Ealing comedy.

Luke Danny used to drink Robert's posh wine and Robert would say to him, "Danny, are you an alcoholic?"

Danny I went through a period of heavy drinking around this time: I drank every night, and I developed a really terrible backache. I saw a doctor at one point and he told me that I was well on the way to damaging my liver, so I didn't drink for two years afterwards. Not a thing. Later, when Thunder had a rider, I realised quite quickly that I would head back down that road if I drank every day, so I made a rule that I would only drink every other day – in other words, half as much as everybody else. I stuck to that rule, too... well, mostly. Nowadays I'm less capable of and less interested in drinking, although when I do drink, I do it to Olympic standards. I say to myself, "Today I am going to get well and truly hammered." It's very infrequent: perhaps once a year. It's done by design rather than by accident, and when I get a hangover, I feel like I've earned it.

Harry Robert was a good guy, but very strange: sort of knowing, and wise about the music business. He obviously approved of me and Nick Linden joining the band, although he didn't really understand the role of the drums. I remember he said to me once, "Harry, I need you to bring in the artillery on the chorus," when anyone else would have said, "Play louder!"

Danny Robert was very good at encouraging us. He used to tell us that getting opportunities to impress audiences were hard to find, so the last thing you wanted in that situation was to fail to do just that. When you leave the stage, they have to know who you are. He gave us so many pearls of wisdom, and I'm sure I must tell someone about them almost every day. We owe him a lot. The older I get, the bigger that debt gets in my mind. He taught us how to conduct ourselves as artists, and never to make a promise that we couldn't keep. These were life lessons, not just relevant to the music industry.

Luke Robert was very keen for me to write original songs, because we'd done covers before that. He said, "Ray Davies wrote his own songs, and you must write songs too!" The first song I wrote was back in 1976 and it was awful. It was called 'Man In The Sky' and it was a complete steal of 'Sweet Home Alabama' meeting 'Freebird'. It was all teenage angst: does God really exist? Why are we here? And so on. But once I got the bit between my teeth, I started writing songs all the time.

Robert wasn't a musician, but he could pick bits of the songs and say, "That's good: say more about that" or "That's bloody rubbish, don't talk about it", and he became quite a taskmaster, but he could see us responding to his guidance. Who knows what he saw in us? Maybe he noticed the chemistry between Danny and me.

Malcolm Robert was an interesting guy, a sort of tall, hawk-like, aristocratic man. The Kinks wrote the song 'Well Respected Man' about him. I always got on well with him, because I had a business mind.

Danny He sent me to see a singing teacher at one point, a posh lady who made me sing scales for about 20 minutes. After that she said, "Here's your money back. I can't teach you anything." Half of me was pleased and the other half was slightly perplexed, thinking that surely I couldn't know everything about singing. Thinking about it now, she probably thought I was a hopeless case. I've always paid a lot of attention to the physicality of my voice. I'm sure all singers are probably aware of it – after all, you don't strap on a voice like you do a guitar. I wish I'd had more lessons and learned the mechanics of how it all works. I just took it all for granted. It might have saved me a lot of anxiety over the years that followed if I had.

Luke Robert paid for us to go into Parkway Studios in Islington in 1980 and we recorded four songs, all of which were pretty awful, apart from one blues song which wasn't bad in a Led Zeppelin sort of way. I remember him giving Danny a bollocking once: he said, "I'm paying for you to record your songs and you're not fucking trying. You shouldn't be singing low, you should be singing high!" He taught us never to be in a rush – whether to talk to a record company or to top a bill. Always act within your means and wait until you're ready. And he taught us that nothing ever happens the way you want it to happen.

Danny We started a soul band called Danny & The Doo Wops on New Year's Eve, 1980. We've never actually acknowledged that we were actually in the band. We just pretended that they were our mates. Which, of course, they were. Whoops, there goes my split personality again...

Martin Danny was obviously the lead vocalist, Luke played rhythm guitar and Nick Linden played lead guitar. Everybody swapped instruments. We played quite a few gigs, the Tramshed among them. The line-up was me as Eddie Spaghetti, Luke as Otis Blue, Danny as Danny Ocean, Harry as Mojo Filter, Chris Hussey as Belmont Cyclone and Ben was Reverend Fingers Bonehead. Their friend Rudi Riviere also assumed the role of Rocky Tavares, singer and lothario. He mostly oozed, with the occasional bit of singing.

Danny It was unbelievably cheesy, and relied completely on the audience being blind drunk, of course.

Harry It was a bit of fun and a distraction. How many other bands would do a thing like that? I really enjoyed picking up the bass guitar for those shows. Maybe it was the fact I wore a wig too. I don't know...

Danny I started to really enjoy performing as well as the singing. I'd get myself into such a trance onstage that I couldn't remember what had happened afterwards. The others would all be talking about what a great gig it had been, and I had no idea. It was the adrenaline; I'd throw myself around the stage, doing anything to make sure the punters clapped their hands and had a good time.

I can organise it better now, but back then it was more like an animal instinct: a base need. I had to have them jumping up and down. Robert encouraged it. He instilled that in me, although I didn't need much winding up. The problem was that by the end of the show I would be mentally and physically destroyed. It was really bizarre. I never told the rest of them. It's different now: I'm much better at dealing with it. And as the stakes got higher, I learned to rein it in so I had enough voice to sing night after night. It's not easy to do, and I still struggle with controlling it sometimes.

You carry quite a heavy burden as the singer. My first waking thought on the tour bus every day is "How the fuck am I going to do it again tonight?" Because I'm in such a state the next day – physically, mentally and vocally. The band know that I struggle. I have to spend the whole day convincing myself that I can do it. It's very wearing: the longer a tour goes on, the heavier that weight becomes. It's a bit like love and hate at the same time.

1981—1988

A NEW BAND, TERRAPLANE, RISES FROM THE ASHES OF THE BLACKHEATH ROCK SCENE. PLUNGED INTO A PERILOUS WORLD OF RECORD DEALS AND DECIDEDLY ODD MANAGERS, THE CHAPS SUPPORT MEAT LOAF AND PLAY READING BEFORE IT ALL COMES TUMBLING DOWN...

Luke In 1981, we took the next step and formed Terraplane. This was me, Danny, Nick Linden from White Noize and Harry from Moon Tier. Robert Wace was our manager. The name Terraplane was Robert's idea: it's a kind of American car.

Ben Luke was very unpopular for a while on the Blackheath scene because he split up the three bands. Cleverly, he took the talent that he required for Terraplane: it was a very smart move. The best drummer was Harry and the best bassist was Nick, so he recruited them and eliminated the competition in one move.

Harry It caused a few problems locally, because Nuthin' Fancy had to get rid of their rhythm section, and the Moon Tier guys hated both them and me. That whole social scene shut down for a long while, although everyone's friends now.

Luke I upset the apple cart a bit! It was a bit messy, but I wanted to move on because Nuthin' Fancy weren't really going anywhere. Admittedly, we'd released a single on Robert's label, Dynamic Cat Records, which sounded very like Free and sells for about £200 nowadays. I remember getting my copy in great excitement but being very crestfallen to see that the songs were credited to 'Luke Morkey'!

Ben I formed a band called Fortune with Rob and Andy from White Noize, and I got a job as a gofer at Sonet Records in Notting Hill Gate. I worked my way up the ranks, learning every aspect of the music industry. They later bought a recording studio in

For 1937 . . . Hudson's Completely New
TERRAPLANE
" Handsome, isn't it ? "   " Yes . . . and a handsome performer too."
FROM £ 285

Chiswick and had no one to run it, so they threw the keys at me and said, "Go and find out how it works." Here I met Kenny Denton, an amazing engineer and producer: he became my mentor and a lifelong friend. I ended up recording a lot of demos with my friends there. I didn't know at the time, but it was the start of a career in engineering that I continue to this day, although I do less of it these days because, in the Pro Tools era, everyone is a bedroom engineer.

Chris In the early Eighties I was in a band called Robert Hart & The Machine, who were signed to Island Publishing. Somebody decided it might be a good idea for us to participate in a US TV talent show called *Star Search*. Off we went to Los Angeles, where not only were we forced to mime to our song in front of the production team and the entire cast of hopefuls *without our instruments* – just picture that for a minute – we then went on to score the lowest points ever recorded on the programme, being beaten soundly by a nine-year-old Japanese tap dancer. Wave and smile for the cameras as you walk off the stage in defeat, boys... wave and smile.

Harry Luke and Danny were looking to change a few things in their own band, and asked if I wanted to come along. They were the best band of the three in my opinion, so when I got the call from Luke, I thought I should go for it. Funnily enough, my dad thought it was the wrong thing to do at the time because he felt it was a sideways step, but I convinced him that Luke and Danny were different: they had something about them. I could see them going all the way in the music business. Obviously I got that one right.

Above: From one "handsome performer" to another. An advert for the Terraplane built by the Hudson Motor Car Company of Detroit, Michigan between 1932 and 1938.
Right: March 1982 and the Bouncing Ball Disco is clearly the place to be if you want to catch Nuthin' Fancy under the new guise of Terraplane.

BOUNCING BALL DISCO
43 PECKHAM HIGH STREET, S.E.15

OPEN FRIDAY and SATURDAY. — **SUNDAY**
10 p.m. - late. Adm. £2.50   7 - 12. Adm. £2.00

Every Thursday
100% HEAVY ROCK

Thursday, 11th March
MIDNITE MOVIES

Thursday, 18th March
NUTHIN FANCY (NEW NAME TERRAPLANE)

Thursday, 25th March   £1.00
DUMPHIES RUSTY NUTS

Thursday, 1st April
MOONTIER

★ **GUEST D.J.**   *Members must be properly dressed to avoid embarrassment*

FRIDAY & SATURDAY 'Admission Free' before 11 p.m.
DISCO ONLY

Luke Harry made a huge difference to us. Now we had a really hard-hitting, solid drummer. A lot of drummers can't keep time, but he's like a fucking metronome. And he was confident, too: he knew he was good. I remember the first gig we did with him; afterwards he asked where his money was, and we said, "Money?" because we were getting paid peanuts. It turned out that Moon Tier had been paying him all this time, but we explained that at this stage we were all about the joy of making music... To his credit, he understood where we were coming from.

Nick Terraplane rehearsed at my parents' house in Blackheath: the support they gave us was unbelievable. They soundproofed a double garage for us and we rehearsed in there three or four times a week.

Luke At the time I was a warehouse manager on £120 a week, but after a while Robert got us some gigs at Dingwalls clubs up and down the country, and of course I'd be taking sick days off work so we could travel, and in the end they sacked me. But we were moving forward: we supported a lot of bands at the Marquee in late 1981 and early 1982, and as a result of that we were put on the bill at the Reading Festival that year.

Harry At the Dingwalls shows, the lack of budget dictated that the band should take turns sleeping in the back of our van. Unluckily for me, my turn took place during one of the coldest nights of that year. The boys cleared the snow and opened the back of the van, and I emerged, looking very blue and close to death... How's your luck!

Danny I'm not sure which year it was, but I do remember very clearly the day we went from being a support band at the Marquee to being a headliner. The venue manager Nigel called me one afternoon and asked if

we could get 50 people to the venue that night. If we could, we would henceforth be headliners. It turned out the band he had booked had sold no tickets and had pulled

out, so he needed a stand-in. We'd been begging him for a headline slot for ages, so it was a great chance for us. I said I'd have to check if the band could do it, then come back to him. I rang round and we agreed we'd go for it and see what happened, so we called everyone we knew, and in the end we got over 200 in there. Nigel was chuffed to pieces, and we were headliners. A momentous day. The band that pulled out? They were called Big Country.

Harry We played the Reading Festival on August 29, 1982, opening on the Sunday. Now that was amazing! I remember thinking at the time that I needed to do more of these bigger gigs.

Chris I had been in a band with a vocalist called Robert Hart (as in Robert & The Machine), who went on to sing for Bad Company. He shared a manager with Go West, who were, at the time, one of my favourite bands. The management contacted me and asked if I'd be prepared to audition for Go West for a forthcoming world tour. I dutifully bit his hand off and successfully started rehearsals with them for a 'probationary period', during which time the tour was postponed. After a couple of months of waiting around for news, I finally had a call to say they'd decided I wasn't right and had given me the 'Spanish archer'.

This was my first big taste of disappointment, made worse by finding out they had been auditioning for weeks before they decided to tell me. That's the music business for you! One of the secrets of a long career as a musician is having the tenacity and enough belief in yourself to shake off setbacks like that.

Ben I followed Terraplane a year later, playing the Reading Festival in 1983 with Fortune. Black Sabbath headlined with Ian Gillan singing. They brought a 45-foot-high polystyrene Stonehenge set with them: the inspiration for the infamous *Spinal Tap* scene.

Luke I found a bill from the Reading Festival the other day. They paid us £75 and we paid them £46 to hire the drum riser! But it was great, considering we were the first band on. Robert had given us lots of interesting observations about our live show. He said, "Don't be in a hurry to get to the end of a song – if you hit a good groove, keep it going. If the guitar solo is going well, keep it going." He told Danny to stand still more, because you draw the audience's attention that way and when you do move, they go wild. He was absolutely right: really good frontmen know that trick. Also, if you run around you run out of breath, which doesn't help your singing.

Above: The legendary Robert Wace, manager of Terraplane from 1980 to 1987, and a flyer for the 1982 Reading Festival, where Danny and Luke returned, this time to perform.
Opposite: The Reading Festival settlement. It seemed like a lot of money for a drum riser...

national rock festival
an njf/marquee presentation

90 Wardour Street, London W1
telephone 01 437 6601

TERRAPLANE :   £75 . 00 .

Less drum riser
paid on your behalf   46 . 00

                             £ 29 . 00

· Thanks for a great set —
next year top of the bill and
the cheque may be for £29,000! †
                    Best Wishes

                    Myra Hickey .

In 1982 Robert went to the States and played some of our demos to John Carter, who was an A&R man at Capitol in LA. Carter obviously saw something there and suggested that we demo some songs for Capitol at Abbey Road in Studio 2, where The Beatles had made all their albums! That was amazing, although we didn't know what we were doing so we were completely in other people's hands. When Carter arrived in the UK he summoned me to his hotel so I could play him the songs. I went on the bus with my acoustic guitar in a black bin liner, as I couldn't afford a case. I felt very out of place waiting in the lobby of the Grosvenor with my guitar in a plastic bag... He said "Nice case!" and gave me some useful advice about the songwriting.

Around that time I was starting to become more proficient with songwriting: it all started to make more sense. We had our first feature in a music magazine in 1982 – it was in the *Melody Maker*, written by a guy called Brian Harrigan who came to Nick's folks' house in Blackheath, where we used to rehearse. He wrote a nice little feature about us.

In late 1982 Robert brought down an engineer called Guy Bidmead from Britannia Row Studios, because he was good friends with Roger Waters of Pink Floyd, who owned the studios. We liked Guy: he was very positive, and he

THE 'PLANE TRUTH

TERRAPLANE deafen Brian Harrigan (again). Pic: Andrew Linden

> **THEY GAVE US MONEY TO BUY COPIES OF OUR OWN SINGLE. I REMEMBER RENTING A SMALL PEUGEOT 205 AND DRIVING AS FAR NORTH AS BIRMINGHAM, BUYING IT FROM DIFFERENT SHOPS ON A LIST.**

liked a drink, which was good. He also drove a Porsche and had a very beautiful girlfriend, so we were impressed. We went up to Britannia Row and demoed another three songs, one of which was 'I Survive', the first thing I ever wrote that I thought was a proper song. It has a good chorus and middle eight, and everything works within it. Capitol passed, unfortunately, but we were approached by Martin Costello of Bayswater Music in 1983. They had an independent label called City Records, and they offered us our first publishing deal. City put out 'I Survive' as a single.

Danny They gave us money to buy copies of our own single. I remember renting a small Peugeot 205 and driving as far north as Birmingham, zigzagging my way across the M1 and M6, buying it from different shops on a list. We all had a list, and we bought loads of copies. I'm not sure where the list came from, but I think the single went into the chart somewhere

around number 46. Naughty as you like, of course, but we were still well excited – and, more importantly, the chart position put us on CBS Records' radar. Ironic really, as they'd turned us down twice already.

Nick We started to hang out with the journalists. The press cuttings we got were really down to Luke and I ligging. Pete Makowski was around, as was Garry Bushell, and quite a few of the other *Sounds* writers were about. It was the best time of our lives: we had such a good laugh, and we were all really good mates. There were never any rows or anything.

Mark Harris Malcolm McKenzie's older brother Ian was my best friend at university, and he had a house in south-east London. I shared the house with Malcolm. Through him I met Luke and Nick in a pub called the Princess of Wales in Blackheath in November 1983. I met Danny the same night, or at least the same week, and Harry shortly afterwards. I socialised with those guys regularly from that point onwards.

Luke Nick and I were the social animals of the group and we used to hang around in London. At this stage, Terraplane would play gigs here and there, but nothing that resembled a real tour was on the horizon.

Mark In terms of staying out late in the West End or wherever, me and Luke and Nick and Malcolm did most of it. Harry did a bit less and Danny did even less than Harry,

Above: A photo from Terraplane's first feature in *Melody Maker*, 1982.
Right: Shenanigans outside a sex shop in Lewisham in 1982.

because he was always working hard in the daytime. We'd check out bands in the old Marquee and disappear into the 'Wardour Street triangle', as we called it, between the Ship, the Marquee and the St Moritz Club.

Luke I wrote a letter to Garry Bushell at *Sounds* and he liked our tape, and as a result he came to watch us play a pub gig in Maidenhead and wrote a glowing review. That, together with the City single, started things moving a bit and we sold out the Marquee for the first time in late 1983. Not long after that I decided that we needed a second guitarist, so I asked my mate Tony to play with us. Robert had organised a showcase gig for the record companies at the Marquee in early 1984, although we had no idea if any of them would come along.

Danny Someone at the CBS label phoned Luke up, asking if he could come to the showcase, but he was in the bath.

Luke It was a guy called Nicky Graham, who was in A&R at CBS. He had somehow heard the City single and it had created an impression, so he wanted to come and see us.

Danny Luke's mum banged on the bathroom door and told him that CBS were on the phone. He told her it was probably Harry mucking about, and that she should tell him to sod off. She went down and said into the phone, "Sod off, Harry!" Nicky said, "I don't know who you think I am, but I'm from CBS, and we do want to come to the gig. Is it possible to talk to Luke?" Luke's mum went back and told him, "He's adamant that he's from CBS."

Luke I was convinced that it was someone playing a joke on me. We'd been in touch with CBS before this, and at the time they weren't interested.

Danny Luke said "Right!", climbed out of the bath, put a towel on and came downstairs, really angry. He was convinced it was Harry, because CBS had turned us down twice already. He said to the guy, "If this is a joke, you're going to die," and Nicky Graham said, "No, I am who I say I am. We are CBS and we'd like to come and see you play at the Marquee." Luke said, "Oh right... how many people?", and the guy told him 20. Luke answered, "Twenty people! That's our whole guest list." In the end we told Robert that we needed 20 on the guest list, but we didn't tell the other guys in the band. We were concerned they might go all wobbly if they knew there were that many record company people judging us.

Luke We did the gig, which was amazing, with Tony on guitar.

Danny When CBS came down to the gig, they zoomed right in on Tony, because there weren't many black guys playing rock guitar at the time. It was a sales point for them: they made a really big deal out of it.

Luke Two days later CBS said they wanted to sign us for the sum of £75,000! Immediately I asked Tony if he wanted to quit his job at MFI and join us. I assumed he'd jump up and down and say yes, but instead he said, "No, it's not for me." Why? That's a very good question. Maybe he didn't want to leave his job. Also, he had his own band, so maybe he wanted to make it his own way.

Danny Tony wouldn't do it – he had his own band, Moon Tier. I could feel this record deal, that I'd waited nine years to get, collapsing around my ears. I went to Robert and said, "It's no good. We'll have to tell CBS that Tony's not in the band after all." And CBS said, "If there's not five of you in the band, we'll reduce the advance to £50,000." They knocked 25 grand off and wanted us to promise to get another black guitarist! They literally specified that he had to be black. It was unbelievable. We said, "No, if we get a guitarist it'll be because he's the best man for the job."

Nick We signed to Epic, which was part of CBS, in 1984. Getting that deal was amazing: one of those moments in life when you can't believe it. A few weeks later we were being picked up in limos to play *Saturday Superstore* and then going on tour with Meat Loaf. At that age, what more could you want?

Luke Fifty grand felt like a fuck of a lot of money, but in the Eighties there was so much money in the music business. We had a drinks party at Nick's house and invited all our parents.

Danny When we signed to CBS, I gave up a really good carpeting business. I had a contract to supply all the carpet fitters to a rather large and famous carpet store in Lewisham. I was making plenty of money. Giving that up meant plunging myself back into financial insecurity. We'd been trying to get a record deal for nine years, and been rejected by every label in London, sometimes more than once, but this was a big deal and we had to go for it. We were sure it would work out well. After all, CBS was a major label – it had to work out, didn't it? Wrong again.

My dad was not convinced, and advised me not to sell my tools. He was partly right, and I didn't sell them.

Harry Signing the record deal was a dream come true, and a great excuse to quit my day job.

Ben While all this was going on, I was a full-time studio engineer. In 1984 I recorded with George Michael: he was singing backing vocals on a single for his cousin. 'Careless Whisper' had just been a big hit and he was a huge star at the time. I was astounded by his musical ability: he worked on a mundane song for 45 minutes, changed the melodies around, and by the end of that time it sounded like a hit. My dining-out story is that George was hungry and wanted to buy some food from the shop over the road, but he didn't have any money on him so I lent him a fiver – I never got it back!

Chris During the early Eighties I spent a lot of time in resident bands playing chart music, which I guess contributed to me being a bit of a musical chameleon. I also auditioned for a number of acts, Bananarama and Howard Jones being two of them, but never really got the break I was looking for. I was put forward for an audition with Mick Ralphs' new band after he parted ways with Bad Company, and during the try-out, which had Chris Slade from AC/DC on drums, Dave Gilmour dropped in to jam with us. I didn't take the gig, which in retrospect was probably as stupid as not taking the gig with Nik Kershaw.

I moved to Cardiff to work in the Top Rank and picked up a huge amount of TV work, eventually becoming part of the band behind a local duo called Waterfront. They signed with a major company and we recorded an album that eventually went Top 10 in the US, leading to my first ever tour – three months coast to coast across America supporting Donny Osmond. Despite appearing on *Top Of The Pops*, the band never made it in the UK, and eventually disappeared.

Danny In early 1985, Terraplane supported Meat Loaf. Big shows, arenas. We went to Ireland and I became very sick with the flu and tonsillitis. I missed a couple of shows and stayed in bed for three days. An old Irish doctor called Fergus Brady, who

looked like someone out of *Father Ted*, came to see me and told me that I had 'senile tonsils', where your tonsils are constantly flooding your body with toxins. He said that I had to get rid of them, and that having them removed wouldn't affect my singing voice. The label weren't having it. Neither was the manager. I even saw a Harley Street ENT surgeon who'd operated on opera singers, and I got him to write me a note explaining it all. Nothing doing; they still refused point-blank. They said they had a lot of money tied up in my voice and weren't prepared to take the risk. We'd waited so long to get a record deal, and we'd been through so much, I eventually let it go. I shouldn't have, but I did. I was constantly ill, and always had some antibiotics on me – I practically lived on the buggers. It was miserable.

Luke We got Rudi Riviere on board as a second guitarist in time for the Meat Loaf tour in early 1985, and not because he was black: it was because he was a great guitar player and we liked him.

Nick That tour was fun. I was seeing Meat Loaf's bassist's sort-of girlfriend, and he got his own back on me by detuning my bass while I was playing. All that young man stuff was going on.

Luke The Meat Loaf tour was great. There was a professional road crew and the whole thing was a step upwards. As a result I felt like a professional for the first time, even though we were staying in horrible guest houses every night. Well, I wasn't: I struck up a relationship with Meat Loaf's backing singer Kati, and so I got to stay in their hotel! I remember one night witnessing a terrible row between him and his wife, who had flown from the USA to see him: she was standing there in her underwear, swearing at him.

TERRAPLANE

Meatloaf tour Itinerary

January · 16th Manchester Apollo   ⎫ CANCELLED
         17th Leicester De Montford Hall ⎭
         19th Newcastle City Hall
         20th Edinburgh Playhouse
         22nd Manchester Apollo
         23rd Birmingham NEC
         24th Harrogate Centre
         26th Bournemouth Windsor Rooms
         27th Brighton Centre
         29th Preston Guildhall
         30th Sheffield City Hall
         31st Ipswich Gaumont

February 2nd Hammersmith Odeon
          3rd   "
          4th   "

          6th Ipswich Gaumont
          7th Manchester Apollo
          8th Newcastle City Hall
         10th Preston Guildhall
         12th – 20th Northern Ireland + Eire

Nick I remember when we met Meat Loaf for the first time: he made a grand entrance, kicking open the door to the room we were in. Unfortunately, two guitars and a bass were behind the door and were knocked over. He was embarrassed, and so were we, so we didn't talk to him again until the last night of the tour.

He had a guitarist called Bob Kulick with him at the time, who was bald with a moustache, and that night I put a bald wig and a fake moustache on, picked up a guitar and went into Meat Loaf's dressing room. He came in and I said, "When are we going on, mate?" and he looked at me, obviously thinking, "What the fuck are you doing?" He didn't say anything and I walked out. Maybe you had to be there.

Danny During the day of the last show of the tour in Ipswich, Nick, Harry and I shat on a plate and left it in Meat Loaf's dressing room, surrounded by a nice arrangement of salad. It was payback for the smashed guitars. Disgusting, of course, but he deserved it.

Luke We got our first front cover during the Meat Loaf tour: it was with *Sounds*. It was all happening now: Mike Read played our first single, 'I Can't Live Without Your Love', on the Radio 1 Breakfast Show, and said, "I think it's going to be a hit" – although, of course, it wasn't. It never got playlisted at Radio 1.

Harry When Terraplane started to become successful, it was wonderful. We performed on *Saturday Superstore* on October 26, 1985, which was a fun experience, although the record company got a stylist in who dressed me in a leopard-skin waistcoat. Very strange. They also changed my haircut: originally I had a curly perm, like everyone else did in the early Eighties. Kevin Keegan's got a lot to answer for. But CBS said it had to go. I thought, "I'm up for a laugh, let's go for it." I was left with nothing but a small blob of hair on top.

Luke CBS wanted us to record a debut album, so we had to find a producer. Our A&R man, Gordon Charlton, took us to a meeting with his boss Muff Winwood. Muff was the former bass player of The Spencer Davis Group, and the brother of Steve Winwood: he was a really nice guy. Muff wasn't always right about things, as we found

out, but he understood music and introduced us to Glyn Johns, who had a recording studio on a farm in Sussex, which we visited. We got on with him but it didn't work out, so we were introduced to a producer called Liam Henshall, who we instantly liked.

He was managed by Red Bus Studios, who had had quite a lot of success with the Culture Club albums, and he had all these plans for where and how to produce the album, which was brilliant. So we got stuck into the first Terraplane album and learned a lot from Liam. He was from an engineering background and I hung out with him a lot, as the guy with the most interest in all that stuff. He was very into cutting-edge synths and other things that we had no experience of, and we had a great laugh.

Harry Recording the album, which we called *Black And White*, was a high point, although Liam Henshall wanted a harsh sound from the cymbals. He called it a 'you cunt' sound, so I only used china cymbals rather than crashes or rides.

Luke Everything on that album sounds like we've had 28 cups of coffee – totally energetic. It came out in 1985 and that summer we did a club tour. We got Dave 'Bucket' Colwell, who was later in Bad Company, to play second guitar.

Nick The first Terraplane album was very much what we were about: raw, heavy rock. The second one, *Moving Target*, wasn't quite as good. It came out in 1987 and by then CBS and Robert were encouraging us to wear some pretty embarrassing clothes. It was the mid-Eighties: a horrible time for rock music, really.

Mark The record company didn't know what to do with a bunch of south London rockers, and the guys themselves hadn't reached the stage where they were assertive enough to say, "Sorry, we're not dressing like that."

Luke I tried writing a few songs with Phil Pickett, a nice guy who had worked with Sailor in the Seventies and then had a huge amount of success with Culture Club in the Eighties. He ended up producing the second album and it was very lightweight indeed, so any credibility we'd had was instantly destroyed!

Nick The music lost its soul on the second album, which was very overproduced. It was partly down to the producer Phil Pickett, who was experimenting a bit. It was recorded at Trident Studios 1 and 2, though, which was amazing.

Luke No regrets. You have to take responsibility for the bad decisions you make, and we were on a steep learning curve. Also, I came out of that album experience pissed off, and it definitely had an effect on the subsequent songs that I wrote. It was almost as if we needed to go that far in the wrong direction to come back in the right one.

Danny If you assume that the record company know what they're doing, that's your first, and possibly your biggest, mistake. It took us three more years of making decisions with our heads rather than our hearts before we learned that lesson. They were the mighty CBS, for fuck's sake. I'd waited nine years for this, and it eventually dawned on me that we'd messed it up by believing in them rather than in our own instincts. It was a tough thing to accept, but proved to be a valuable lesson for later on.

Luke One of the problems with the relationship between our band, Robert Wace and CBS was that we had no clear musical direction. CBS were very much a pop label: they had Wham!, Sade and so on. Their whole operation was about pop and how to market it, whereas our next label, EMI, was a rock label, with Iron Maiden and Marillion and so on. Despite leaning very much towards rock, we were always being reined in, with them saying,

"Oh, that guitar sound is a bit heavy, it needs to be a bit more poppy – and maybe you should have your hair cut this way."

It was the label people who were saying this stuff, from Muff Winwood down to the marketing staff, and Robert had been out of the loop for a while so he'd lost some of the old arrogance he'd had in the Sixties. And we didn't know ourselves what we were trying to do exactly. Add to this our producer Liam Henshall, who was as eclectic as hell, and the results were confused to say the least. We'd got through the first album, but by the second one it was starting to go downhill. After the Meat Loaf tour there were a few gigs on the horizon, but it was all a bit of a struggle. We knew something wasn't quite right, but we weren't sure what.

Danny We never made much money in Terraplane. We did buy some flight cases for our first tour. They cost three grand. We've still got some of them.

Harry We played the Reading Festival again in 1987. We'd done our second album, *Moving Target*, the same year, and it really wasn't a rock album. It was totally the wrong direction for a band like us, although I think it still sounds good nowadays. I don't think we were well received by the audience, though. They were throwing bottles of piss at us, which I didn't really like. Well, you wouldn't, would you?

Luke There were so many keyboards on *Moving Target* that we had to get a keyboard player for the subsequent dates: a guy called Scott Davidson, who, thanks to a recommendation from me, got a job with Bros!

Harry With hindsight, the big picture was that we were listening to the wrong advice and Terraplane was coming to an end. The record company wanted hits, so they wanted us to soften the sound. The first and second albums sound like they were recorded by two different bands.

Danny In 1987, I'd had enough and decided I had to have my tonsils removed, with or without the consent of the label. They were infected all the time, and pouring poison down my throat, which was

lowering my immunity. I'd become seriously fed up with constantly being ill, so I phoned the doctor and said that I wanted to see a specialist.

I saw an ENT guy called Dr Salmi, who looked down my throat and winced. He said he'd never seen tonsils that bad, and gave me a date for the operation there and then: it was a few weeks later, in early February 1988. The label had decided to re-release 'If That's What It Takes', one of our singles. Ironically, the operation was set for the same date as the single release. I told Luke and he was a bit twitchy, but I was

PAGE 4 PIN UPS!

pretty pissed off about it all, and certain they'd get no joy with the single. He said, "What happens if they get us on *Top Of The Pops*?" I said, "I'm pretty sure they won't, but if they do, you'll just have to get someone to impersonate me, because I've got to do this."

Six months later, I woke up one day and felt really well, for the first time in years. I couldn't believe how great I felt. I came to the conclusion that my system was finally free of all the tonsil misery. Band-wise, the relationship with CBS had broken down, and it was clear that we needed to have a good think about where we were going.

After the second album came out, we had a meeting with Muff Winwood, our A&R man. Luke said, "Muff, I think we've made the wrong record: we should have made a rock record and we've made a pop record." Muff

said, "I think you might be right." By this time we'd all had our hair chopped off at the record company's request. We were trying very hard to be acceptable, but we were caught between two stalls: we weren't a rock band, and we certainly weren't a pop band. We were starting to realise this now.

We told Muff that we wanted to make a much rockier album the next time, and he said, "You might have to grow your hair a bit, though." At that exact point I realised how little he understood about our band. It was all I could do not to leap across the table and strangle him, but I bit my tongue and said,

"It's growing as we speak!" He said, "Great!" He had no idea I was taking the piss. When we got outside afterwards, we agreed it was obvious that our days with CBS were numbered, and though it wasn't official, the record deal was effectively over.

By this time I didn't even know whether I wanted to be in a band any more. I was very angry, and pissed off with record companies, managers, everyone really, but mostly with myself.

Left: The 7" shaped picture disc of 'If That's What It Takes'.
Above: An early shoot for Epic in which we were joined by Rudi Riviere (second from right). The writing's on the wall: look at our expressions!

41

1988—1990

DETERMINED NOT TO ACCEPT DEFEAT, A NEW BAND FORMS. THUNDER (FOR IT IS THEY) MAKE A COLOSSAL EARLY IMPACT, DOMINATING DONINGTON 1990 AGAINST ALL THE ODDS.

Danny In April 1988, Luke and I went to New York and LA to stay with people we knew, as a way to get in touch with what we thought we needed to do. My dad lent me some money for the flight and I also maxed out two credit cards to get us there. Harry was working as a part-time travel agent at the time, so he got us one of those round-the-world tickets that you used to get.

Harry Luke and Danny went out to America and realised that Terraplane needed to reinvent itself completely. It was evident that our futures were uncertain and that something needed to change.

Luke Using the contacts we had, we set up a load of meetings in New York and LA. It was the first time we'd been to America, and it was a real eye-opener. We stayed at a flat in Hell's Kitchen which belonged to Kati, Meat Loaf's backing vocalist, who I was no longer in a relationship with but with whom I had stayed friends.

Danny I couldn't believe how buzzing New York was. We went to a place called the Acme Bar & Grill, which had a marked effect on me because all the professional musos were hanging out there. The

drummer who got up to jam was introduced as the guy who'd just finished the latest David Bowie tour. They were all such great players, and jamming free-form shit left, right and centre. I was blown away. It wouldn't have happened in London.

Luke God knows why people took our meetings: we were just two English kids. But giving up was never an option for me. I write songs and I play guitar, and I'm shit at everything else! So we met ICM, the biggest agent of the time, and a couple of labels who thought our music was unimpressive. When we got to LA, we booked into our hotel and went up to the Rainbow. When we left, and drove out of the car park, Danny turned the car the wrong way by mistake and we crashed into oncoming traffic. The police arrived and made him walk the white line: luckily he hadn't had a drink. The next day we got a new hire car and moved into a new hotel, but our room was broken into and a load of cash and cards got stolen!

Danny We had a week in each city and we watched what was going on in the music scene. I remember Luke saying, "We've just got to be a rock band again."

> WE HAD A WEEK IN EACH CITY AND WE WATCHED WHAT WAS GOING ON IN THE MUSIC SCENE. I REMEMBER LUKE SAYING, "WE'VE JUST GOT TO BE A ROCK BAND AGAIN."

Luke The most important part of the trip was when we visited the Sunset Strip in LA. It was the time when Guns N' Roses were blowing up, and all these kids were walking around with big hair and tight jeans. England seemed pretty dour in comparison. There was an energy there which really made an impact on us. We listened to the music and I said to Danny, "The new songs that I'm writing would fit in here much better than they would anywhere else. What we need to do is what we should have been doing all along – making great rock music."

Danny When we got home, we decided that we needed to change our manager, so we called our friend Liam Henshall, who produced the first album and who knew a lot more about the music business than us, and he recommended a few lawyers to see. After our very first meeting with a lawyer, I felt as though the scales had fallen from our eyes. It was apparent that Robert had wrapped us up in cotton wool and protected us, as he saw it, perhaps from things that might make us realise his shortcomings. I don't think he did it deliberately, but it was hard not to be angry when we realised what had happened.

Luke Firing Robert wasn't pleasant, but firing people never is. Danny and I told him that we needed to move on and that we wanted to find someone new to manage us. He said, "So, just because the band isn't doing very well, you want to blame the bloody manager?" – or words to that effect.

Danny Look, Robert was a very old-school manager. He would say, "Leave that to me, dear." We were more into rehearsing and going to the pub and talking about how massive we were going to be, because we were 20 years old. He meant well, and he always looked out for us, but it seemed to us that he was a Seventies man in an Eighties world. I didn't want to be 'protected' from the realities of the business any more, and neither did Luke.

Harry I think Robert went off and got a job with the government. Doing what, I have no idea.

Nick I could see that the CBS deal was coming to an end at that point. We were on a yearly deal initially, and then it went down to six months, and then a month, and then finally a week's retainer. It got ridiculous: CBS weren't promoting anything we did. We asked to be released, and they refused – but eventually they let us go. Fortunately, just before we got dropped, our accountant advised us to buy houses while we still had the means of securing a mortgage.

Luke CBS dropped us, so our next job was to find a new manager.

Malcolm I had observed Terraplane when they were signed to CBS, and I had a lot of questions. We'd go to the Princess of Wales in Blackheath in the evenings – usually me and Luke, sometimes me and Danny – and chat about stuff. We'd ask, "Why do things this way? Why not do them that way?" and so on. Things started to go bad with CBS and I remember thinking that I could definitely manage them. They said to me, "Look, if you think that you've got good ideas, write them down and let's talk about it."

Danny Malcolm had a great job and was making a lot of money, but he'd seen what Robert had done and he knew he could do a better job of it. He came to us and his plan was very well rounded and very well conceived.

Luke Malcolm, Danny and I went out one night to see Lita Ford play at the Marquee. Jon Bon Jovi came onstage to do the encore with her and the place went nuts! I thought, "We're better than this..."

Malcolm After the show Luke said, "We need to talk." So we went to the St Moritz Club, sat down and hatched the entire plan: getting a new bass player, bringing in another guitarist, changing the band name... the whole works. Luke knew exactly what he wanted to do.

Luke I thought, "We need to start all over again." I knew there was a massive audience for rock'n'roll out there. I thought Danny and I needed to start again as a duo: we seriously considered getting rid of Harry, which would clearly have been the wrong thing to do.

Malcolm I basically approached it from a slightly different view to the usual music managers, who are usually slightly dodgy, creative people who are more about plugging records than they are about the business side. It's only when you get much further up the food chain, to the Rod Smallwoods of this world, that you find managers with corporate minds. I was somewhere in between, so I wrote a business plan – which was not something you'd usually see from a music manager. From that, the decision was made that I was going to manage the band, initially as Terraplane. Mark Harris came in as my partner in the management company.

Danny We thought we'd give him a chance to do it. He said, "The experience that I don't have, we'll buy from other people. We'll get ourselves a great lawyer and a great accountant."

Malcolm Here's a good anecdote: I remember Danny and Luke sitting me down and saying, "There's something you need to know. When you go out and talk about our band to people, they will all have an opinion and they will all tell you what they think. When they do, look them in the eye and think – not say, but *think* – 'Don't fucking tell me about my band, because I fucking know better than you do.'" They'd been quite bruised by the whole Terraplane experience. That attitude was helpful, but it was also harmful, because it meant that they were quite shut off from external advice that could have been very good for them.

Danny I've said this many times over the years: what makes us strong also makes us weak. We're all so much wiser, later on, aren't we?

Mark I spent the entire mid-Eighties working and playing very hard, and frequently falling out of nightclubs with Luke at four in the morning. Occasionally I would go and help Terraplane out at gigs, selling T-shirts or just hanging out. It was pretty low-level touring, with a hired van and band members' cars. I was just there for fun, really. Because I worked in financial services, I was good with the money at the end of the night. I also used to put on gigs at college back when I was 17, so I knew a little about the music industry.

Luke As soon as Malcolm became our manager, he was full of really good ideas. He wanted us to get a really good accountant, for starters. He'd come from a sales background and he had a very impressive business plan. He knew how to conduct himself in a business environment, which we really didn't, and he also had a contemporary way of looking at things. He also understood us as people, because he'd known us so long. He was really driven to do it, which was important because Robert had run out of ideas. We'd learned all we could from him.

It was important to me to get it right this time, having had my fingers burned with Terraplane.

Malcolm Danny has always been very savvy, and very sharp about money. I think he would probably acknowledge that he doesn't have a particularly strategic mind: he tends to see things in black and white, and he's not a particularly deep thinker, which Luke is. That's why they work well together.

Danny Yes, that's me all over: no strategic abilities at all, black and white all day long... I'm being sarcastic here, in case it isn't obvious.

Luke I think anyone who thinks it's as simple as 'Luke's the creative one' and 'Danny's the businessman' is oversimplifying things. I think we trust each other's instincts and abilities and we're both capable of being creative and pragmatic.

Andy Taylor Somewhere along the chain of business, someone approached me who was also doing something for Malcolm, their manager. Aerosmith and Guns N' Roses were huge in America and over here, and we were well behind in terms of the rock we were putting on the table. I'd been living and recording in the States all this time, and I had a small window of time when I came back to the UK and met these guys, so I had a very American viewpoint because I'd lived in LA and I knew all those guys. The English contribution was almost nonexistent.

Luke In the summer of 1988 we recorded demos at a little studio somewhere near Gatwick: these were the demos that got Andy Taylor interested in working with us.

Ben They asked me to help engineer these demos, as they didn't really trust the guy who owned the studio. I think I may have played a bit of piano on one of the songs. This was the first time I realised how good these new songs were, and how far from Terraplane they were. Incidentally, I've never been paid for that session...

Malcolm We were introduced to an accountant called Martin Stainton, who allegedly stole three million quid from Rick Wright of Pink Floyd in 1994, but at the time he was well thought of. We took him on and he compiled a list of possible producers, one of whom was Andy Taylor, who he represented. So I had a meeting with Martin and Andy, who wanted to know more about the band. He liked the music, which was a good starting point. At one point Martin said to Andy, "I just need to go over some figures with you. Do you know you've spent over £27,000 in petty cash over the last month?" Andy looked at me and grinned and said, "I don't call that petty!"

Andy I went down to a gig at the Marquee when they were still playing as Terraplane. They had been moulded by CBS into something they weren't: it stuck out like a sore thumb. I thought they should be sounding more like Led Zeppelin than Toto. Luke can write any sort of song he wants, and Danny's voice is obviously incredible. They just didn't have their rock on, the way it should have been on. That's what I thought, and we ended up getting pissed and talking about doing things a different way. They reformatted it, made a few changes, and Luke and I pissed around writing a few little bits and pieces, and we came out with 'She's So Fine' and 'Until My Dying Day'. He also wrote 'Dirty Love', so we had that handful of songs to demo up.

Malcolm Andy was very confident: he'd had a lot of success and didn't give a shit about anything. I think a lot of that attitude rubbed off on all of us; he was a real character and a breath of fresh air.

Danny Taylor saw us very much as the band he wished he'd been in. He said more than once, "It's amazing: you're actually in a band with people you like!" He loved it. He saw where we were lacking, though: we'd had the confidence kicked out of us with all the things that had gone wrong. We were angry, but we weren't angry enough. Taylor saw that, and encouraged us. He was looking for a new challenge: he'd done Rod Stewart's album *Out Of Order* the same year, which was the rockiest album Rod had done in ages, and I loved it. As soon as Stainton mentioned Taylor to Malcolm, I thought, "That might work." We met him and we liked him, and he encouraged us to turn it up.

Luke Any doubts I might have had about the new direction were dispelled the moment I met Taylor at Chipping Norton Studios in Oxfordshire. He came in with sunglasses on, even though it was dark, and I liked him immediately. He had a lot of ideas. After that I went to his flat in Wandsworth and we drank some beer and wrote some songs together: out of that session came 'She's So Fine'.

We did another session with Andy Taylor at Trident 2 Studios in late 1988. Ruby Turner sang backing vocals. I can't remember all the songs we recorded, but among them were 'Dirty Love', 'Dance, Dance, Dance ('Til The Night Is Through)' and 'Stay With Me'. Benny engineered this session and added piano to 'Stay With Me'. Andy also played guitar on that song.

Andy When we recorded 'Dirty Love' and 'She's So Fine', I took the tape home and listened to it and thought, "I don't think I've ever recorded rock music as good as this."

Malcolm They were struggling as Terraplane, and I didn't have any experience as a manager so I knew I needed to learn a bit about the music business. We were looking for lawyers, and we signed up a guy called Howard Jones who was at a law firm called Sheridans. Howard was great: a very serious, well-connected guy who gave up his Thursday evenings for a month to talk about contracts and answer my questions. He basically educated me and became my closest adviser. He was the one who said, "Change the name." He told me that in the music industry, new is shiny and old is tarnished, and that we should keep all but one of the band members.

Nick We used to have a meeting every New Year's Day and work out the plan for the year to come, and on January 1, 1989, Luke and Danny said that we were flogging a dead horse, that we'd been dropped by the label, that we were not going to get signed again, and that it would be better to split the band up. They were going to go off on their own. I understood it, because I could see that the band was coming to an end. You can't get rid of Harry, and Luke and Danny are the writer and the singer, so it probably had to be me who went: there was no other way around it. The public and the press wouldn't have been fooled if Terraplane had simply changed their name. Something more drastic had to happen. Malcolm might have had a little bit of a grudge against me because I took his job: he'd been the bass player in Nuthin' Fancy, after all.

Mark I think it was tough for Nick to be sacked, because he'd been in Terraplane for so long.

Nick I've been married and I've been divorced, but the worst divorce of all was splitting up with those guys. That makes you stronger, though, and I kept my dignity. I still love those guys and I would never put them down in any way.

Luke In January 1989 we recorded more demos at Great Linford Manor Studios in Milton Keynes. The session drummer we'd booked

didn't show up, so we asked Harry to play drums. I played guitar and bass, Andy Taylor produced and Ben engineered.

Harry Initially I wasn't going to be involved in the new band: I think they had another drummer lined up. I didn't mind. I was meandering through life quite happily, but in limbo, and I suppose I would have found another band. But they asked me to go up and do some demos in January 1989, so of course I said I would.

Luke We chose our new band name as a combination of two things: a song called 'Distant Thunder', which I'd written, and the title of Taylor's first solo album. I went to the band, told them my idea for the new name, and they all liked it.

Malcolm Managing a band is the best job and the worst job in the world, as I see it. Don't expect to be thanked: you'll be waiting a long time! You need to be a gofer, a salesperson and a brilliant negotiator. You need to have a good bedside manner and you need to have a good marketing brain. You're

effectively the band's managing director and the band are the shareholders, so you run the band for them, the rest of the board being the record company and the publisher and so on. You can't expect the band – even guys as smart as Danny and Luke – to understand all the issues involved. Of course, they understand them now, because they've been managing themselves for so many years, but 25 years ago that wasn't the case – although, of course, they'd been through a lot with Terraplane.

Harry I was convinced after the Linford Manor sessions that we had something special. The music sounded quite different to anything else.

Malcolm In February we invited a bunch of record companies to come down to our rehearsals in London. What impressed the record companies at the showcases was that we didn't really care. We deliberately set those shows up so that there would be three companies there at the same time, and they could all see each other. Phonogram, Arista, Polydor... they were all there. And we made them pay a contribution to the showcase too!

There had been a review in *Raw* magazine, written by Malcolm Dome, saying that we had recorded a Zeppelin-esque demo, which had piqued the labels' interest. I'd played three tracks for Malcolm Dome, but not given him the tape, on the band's instructions, because everybody wants something that they can't have. The same logic applies to record companies. If they feel privileged to hear something, they place a higher value on it. That was Danny's strategy, and it worked.

> " WE CHOSE OUR NEW BAND NAME AS A COMBINATION OF TWO THINGS: A SONG CALLED 'DISTANT THUNDER', WHICH I'D WRITTEN, AND THE TITLE OF TAYLOR'S FIRST SOLO ALBUM. I WENT TO THE BAND, TOLD THEM MY IDEA FOR THE NEW NAME, AND THEY ALL LIKED IT. "

Harry It felt almost as if we were auditioning the record companies, not the other way round. The session bass player who played with us got very nervous and didn't play well, but we still came across well enough. Job done!

Malcolm All this, combined with Howard Jones' machinations behind the scenes and the fact that Andy Taylor knew a few people, wound up with Thunder getting signed.

Harry Malcolm knew what he was doing. He knew what business decisions to make, and he was a mate too.

Malcolm All the labels were interested except EMI, and on the morning of the last showcase my home phone rang and it was Nick Gatfield from EMI. I knew that Howard Jones had sent Nick our tape, because Nick was one of his closest friends, but that Nick hadn't come back to him, which cheesed Howard off. So I said, "Hi," and he said, "Tell me about this band Thunder." I said, "It's too late, mate," and he said, "What do you mean? It's never too late!" and came along to the showcase and loved it. I think he liked it because we were so offhand about it. Record companies are like masochists: they love getting beaten up. I was so pissed off by all the record labels by that point, I didn't give a shit.

Nick called us in for a meeting the next day and told us, "I like the band, but liking the band is only half of it. What's the plan?" – and fortunately we had one. Within a couple of weeks the deal was signed. We asked for £220,000 on signing, including the cost of the first record, which was budgeted at £145,000. It was a five-album deal.

Andy It was smart of the label to sign the band. Thunder were doing what no one else was doing, and most labels wouldn't even entertain it. But Nick Gatfield wasn't stupid: he saw an opportunity from a British perspective to do what the Americans were doing.

Luke £220,000 felt like a proper deal. You could actually do something with that much money, given the expense of hiring studios and so on. Then the publishers started sniffing around, so we signed a publishing deal and I bought a nice flat in Blackheath with my share of the advance. I put the rest in the bank, which felt really weird, because I'd never been in that position in my life! In Terraplane we'd just scraped by, paying ourselves £200 a month or something. It was a good time to be alive. I said to myself, "I'm actually going to enjoy this, after all the misery and pain."

Andy Every album I produced before Thunder was a platinum album, apart from my solo record, and I'd just done a Rod Stewart LP which sold seven million copies, and before that I'd done Robert Palmer's stuff. I knew what I was doing, but if you don't know how to talk a record executive's language, nothing happens. I had a long relationship with EMI from Duran Duran, though, and I could push things through.

Malcolm We were offered a staggering amount of money for the publishing from EMI Music in America – $250,000 or something stupid like that – but it was a 'life of copyright' deal, and our lawyer warned us that if we signed it we'd be giving up copyright in the songs forever. 'Life of copyright' deals are virtually outlawed in the UK, but in America they still exist. I went to the boys, who were all excited about the $250,000, and I told them about the problem, and they said, "Fine – let's find another publishing company." And we did. They weren't afraid to say no to things, even at that early stage.

We had a signing party at EMI in Manchester Square and drank a lot of beer and champagne. We'd been to School Dinners, the restaurant with a gay headmaster and schoolgirls as waitresses, with Jonathan Green, who was our product manager at the time and went on to be the head of Mercury Records. We had him spanked by the girls. We went back to the offices, absolutely annihilated, and on the way out one of us grabbed these big

pictures of Brother Beyond off the wall and snapped one of their heads off. After that we went off to the West End and had a night of absolute carnage... Of course, I got a phone call from EMI the next day and got bollocked.

Mark Malcolm and I are totally different characters: we're interested in different things. Malcolm was very much the man who fronted things. He's a hunter and I'm a skinner! In other words, he'll decide when he wants to go on tour, and I'll get the budget together, recruit the crew and so on. I was the financial director of the company, so I found the office, made sure the band's bills were paid, checked the details and so on, while Malcolm was much more interested in strategy and negotiations. But when there's two of you, as there were before our colleague Vicky McIvor joined, you have to do a bit of everything. If Malcolm was in America talking to Geffen, for example, I'd be at EMI approving artwork.

Malcolm We agreed early on that the band wouldn't go into the label offices unless they had to, because they wanted to be at arm's length and not be easily reachable by the label. As a consequence, they weren't privy to some of the worst excesses at the record company – and, believe me, we saw some. An example is that some of the senior staff at one particular label were cocaine addicts. They employed a member of staff as a drug dealer; he used to carry the stuff around in cassette cases.

Mark The guys in Thunder had made every mistake possible in Terraplane, so in a sense they'd had a dry run at it already. Malcolm and I had been with them throughout that period, so we understood how the industry worked. When the deal came from EMI, there were very clear decisions made by Thunder about what they would do and what they wouldn't do. They were very clear-cut about that.

Danny By then, we'd been through the sausage machine of one major label and come out the other side. We knew the way they worked, and we were not going to be told how to do our thing. We were very confident in the new music, and we'd agreed with Malcolm how we were going to go about it. If they didn't like it, they could fuck off: it was that simple. Luke has always been very driven, and at that point he was in overdrive, as was I.

Luke We still needed a bass player and a second guitar player. Harry recommended a bassist called Mark Luckhurst from his previous band.

Harry At the beginning of 1989, I was playing in a band called Hellfire Corner, and Mark was the bass player. I told him that Thunder were going to be auditioning bass players soon, and that I thought he'd be good for the band and that he'd do really well.

Mark 'Snake' Luckhurst I was playing sessions in London at the time, auditioning for bands here and there: I auditioned for Adam & The Ants once. I must have done at least 70 or 80 of them over a period of six months, which made me really good at auditioning! I also played with Owen Paul, the songwriter who had a hit in 1986 with 'My Favourite Waste Of Time' – there's footage of me on *Top Of The Pops* with a huge blonde mullet and a bass really high up on my chest!

At the time I auditioned for Thunder, I was playing in a band called Hellfire Corner. Harry was playing drums in that band, and I loved his drumming: he's such a metronome. He asked Luke and Danny to come down and see us, and I had a long chat with them: Danny wanted to get to know me a bit, while Luke wanted to talk music. They asked me to come and audition, so I learned 'She's So Fine' and a couple of other songs and arranged to come down to Terminal Studios in the Elephant and Castle. I got there early, so I thought I'd go and have a pint at the pub next door – and as I walked towards the pub, I saw them sitting outside, having a drink. Harry said, "'Here he comes!'"

I was slightly embarrassed, because I didn't want to be seen going to the pub on the day of an audition, but it didn't matter because they'd had a couple of previous auditionees who weren't very good – and Danny said to the others, "He looks good, so as long as he can play bass, he's in!" Of course, they knew I could play because they'd seen me onstage, and Harry had obviously recommended me, but they needed to see if we would mesh together as a band. And it couldn't have been easier: we fitted together so well. It was never, ever hard work with Thunder, whether it was writing bass parts to Luke's songs, jamming, playing with Harry... it was all really complementary.

Danny We nicknamed him 'Snake Hips' immediately, because he was so skinny and snake-hipped, and then shortened it to 'Snake'. The name stuck.

Luke Snake joined us on May 2, 1989. It might have been difficult for him because he was coming into a room full of people who all knew each other very, very well, with a manager who they knew very, very well. Malcolm didn't get on with Snake at all. They were just different personalities. That happens sometimes. We didn't have the same problem with Benny, who joined us a month later. We'd known Ben since 1979 and he's a very affable, easy-going character, so we knew he'd be a good fit with the band.

Ben I'd played keyboards for Terraplane at their final two shows, one at the Stick Of Rock in Bethnal Green and the other at the Marquee. They had asked me to join them three times over the years: Nick asked me twice, presumably having been sent by the rest of them because he knew me best, and once I was approached by their weird and wonderful manager Robert Wace.

I didn't like the songs they were doing at the time, but I always knew about Danny's ability as a singer. I had always wanted to work with him, so when they asked me to record the Thunder demos, I said yes. The songs were great, and patently not Terraplane. I thought, "Fuck me, this is the

sort of thing Danny should have been singing for the last five years!" Then, when they asked me to join as the second guitar player, it was a no-brainer. I played keyboards too, but only by default, mainly because no one else wanted to do it! For most of the live show, I play guitar, which is the way I like it. I don't like being tied down to one spot.

We played our first gig as Thunder in Southend on July 13, 1989. There were 10 people and a dog there. I spent a lot of time in Southend in the coming years and must have met at least a hundred people who told me they were at that show – liars! It was part of an eight-date tour, opening for Romeo's Daughter and The Groundhogs among other bands. Much to the annoyance of Tony McPhee, we named it the Toilet Tour: the venues were that awful.

Snake Benny and I were on a salary plus per diems, which meant that we were earning quite a lot of money, because we were getting a certain amount from being on the road, plus a wage and per diems. It ended up being a grand a week or thereabouts, and we weren't paying rent or living expenses, so it was a lot of money back then. It'd even be pretty good now.

Malcolm EMI made 1,000 cassettes of the demos and gave them away at the early shows, and then *Raw* magazine came out with a flexi disc on the cover containing three of the songs. That way people would be able to hear the music, and excitement would build in preparation for the release of the album.

Ben The Toilet Tour was hilarious. We went mad. We drank ourselves to oblivion, playing in all these little pubs and clubs up and down England. Unfortunately, a lot of it got filmed: we took a video camera everywhere we went.

JULY 89 LETTER #1

Dear Rock Music Lover,

I am writing to you today to
inform you of the birth of a new band... THUNDER... This is
the new outfit formed from the ashes of Terraplane, who split
up in January this year. The line up of the band is as
follows:- Luke Morley, guitar; Ben Matthews, guitar; Gary
(Harry) James, drums; Mark (Snake) Luckhurst, bass; and Danny
Bowes, vocals. Although the name was announced in some of the
rock press earlier in the year, the line up has only just been
completed. Luke, Harry and Danny were all members of
Terraplane, and Ben and Snake have both played in several
London based bands. Funnily enough, Harry did sessions, (and a
few stints with other bands) after the Terraplane split,
before returning to the team. It seems Danny and Luke were let
down by the session drummer whilst demo-ing new songs, phoned
Harry in a panic (studio time being a bit on the pricey side),
who obliged them with some pretty happenin' drumming, and the
rest, as they say is history!

The band signed a lucrative world-wide recording contract
with EMI records at the end of April, and since then it's been
"all hooters to the grindstone". Recording will take place in
Milton Keynes during August and September, for the band's
debut LP (working title "Back Street Symphony") with
production by Andy Taylor (Duran Duran, Power Station) and
engineering by Mike Fraser (Aerosmith, Bon Jovi, Dan Reed
Network).

In the meantime, you can hear an introductory taster
of THUNDER music on a flexi-disc, free with the next issue of
RAW magazine (out July 12).   CONTINUED OVER

THUNDER

The flexi features excerpts from the demos of three songs (called:- She's So Fine, Until My Dying Day, and Fired Up), all possibles for the LP, scheduled for release in January 90. There may be a single release this Autumn, but the decision won't be made until the LP is finished.

As well as hearing them, you can see the band play their first live shows this month when they play:-
Southend Pink Toothbrush, July 13th.. Milton Keynes Woughton Centre, 14th.. Reading After Dark, 15th.. London Opera On The Green, 17th.. Birmingham Edwards #8, 18th.. Buckley Tivolis, 20th.. Walsall Junction 10, 21st.. Leeds Duchess Of York, 22nd. The band will be supporting on all dates except London, so get there early. Oh by the way, 1,000 copies of a limited edition one track cassette will be given away during the course of the shows. Each tape will be individually numbered (1-1,000) and will not appear anywhere else. Likewise, 1,000 special tour T-shirts will be on sale at £5.00 each, so in time they will both become collectors items, so don't forget to get yours!

As to the future; plans for the LP cover, videos, and touring etc are well under way, so as soon as I get the information, I'll let you know. It's been a while, but I'm glad to be back in the saddle, and galloping into the sunset!

All the best

Sheila

Auntie Sheila

T.I.T.S (THUNDER INFORMATION TRANSMISSION SERVICE)
114 COOMBFIELD DRIVE DARENTH KENT DA2 7LH

Snake The shagging began on the first date of the tour. Later, when I got married, my wife asked me how many women I'd slept with while I was in Thunder, and I told her that once I got to 300, I stopped counting! A lot of those encounters got filmed, too: who knows where that footage is now… And, of course, there were photos of all this stuff, which we would get developed as we moved from town to town. God knows what the staff at the photo shops thought as they processed them. It was all healthy fun.

Mick Wall The first time I came across Thunder was in 1989, and I didn't know they used to be Terraplane, which was funny because I never liked Terraplane. I thought they were all style and no substance, which was unjustified, really. But I had a very good relationship with EMI in those days, and they gave me a four-track cassette with 'Love Walked In' and 'Backstreet Symphony' and 'Dirty Love'. I thought it was amazing. The music had guts and swing and soul: it wasn't like Metallica or Iron Maiden, it was more like the music I'd grown up with, like Thin Lizzy and Bad Company. Danny's voice reminded me of Paul Rodgers, in a totally authentic way. Thunder were streets ahead of the other bands around at the time, so I raved about them in *Kerrang!*

Snake I love Mick Wall. We had a bromance, Mick and I, because we both liked a drink and a laugh. We were a gang, the band and crew. We'd go out and get messed up together.

Mick They were very easy to be around. Danny couldn't stop talking: he was eminently quotable, and very opinionated. For a journalist, that's gold. Luke was Mr Cool: he must have shagged more birds than any rock star I ever met, including Jon Bon Jovi. He just couldn't keep it in his trousers, and in those days it was almost his job not to. Women loved him, and he was one of those guys who is totally at ease in female company. As for Harry, for me the truly great rock drummers are John Bonham, Keith Moon and him. I thought he was that good. Benny was cute and added a lot to their live sound. Snake was a good mate, but a man apart, I thought, because the other four had all known each other for years.

Ben When we were up onstage the performances were so full of energy. We really put everything into the show, mainly to try and impress the women in the front row. It was fairly chaotic in those early days – let's just leave it at that.

Mick This was five years before Oasis, but they and Thunder were similar in that the guitarist wrote the songs, and he had an amazing frontman to sing them for him. I thought they were unstoppable, and that they would be the next Led Zeppelin. Me and *Kerrang!*'s photographer Ross Halfin went all around Europe with them.

Snake Northern Ireland was pretty eye-opening. I remember playing the King's Hall in Belfast and the security were all dressed in black combat clothing: somebody told me they were the IRA, and for that reason we'd be safe. Later, MTV were with us and they came up with the great idea of getting their cameraman to run along the A1, which runs between Northern Ireland and Eire, with a giant camera on his shoulder, not realising: a) that it's illegal to walk on that road; and b) that the camera looked like a rocket launcher. So the cameraman got out of the van and was swamped with soldiers. We were all laughing like idiots. That was a bit of a learning curve…

Danny We went into Great Linford Studios in Milton Keynes in August 1989 to record our first album, *Backstreet Symphony*. We lived and ate dinner in the big house and recorded in the little studios on the other side of the grounds. Mike Fraser was the engineer and Andy Taylor was producing. Benny's quote is the best. He said that making the first album was a bit like being at a party where an album broke out every now and then.

Andy I suppose I get my pat on the back for turning them into a rock band. We brought in Mike Fraser to do the engineering, with his classic rock chops. I'd used a lot of American guys in my past, like the Power Station engineers from New York, and they always complemented the English sound: it went right back to Zeppelin, who used American engineers. Mike had a lot of experience of dealing with big characters in bands, just as I did, so we worked really

well together. Danny and Luke and Harry are all massive characters, and getting all that on tape is what it's all about.

Harry The booziest time, for me personally, was when we recorded the first album. On tour, if booze is readily available, sometimes you're not bothered by it. I'll never be an alcoholic: I throw up, literally everywhere.

Andy I won't go into the kind of thing we went into in overtime, for legal reasons… Ha ha! As clichéd as it is, when you work that hard, a little bit of relief is needed. That said, Thunder were the cleanest band ever. They never touched coke, and they didn't even smoke dope. All they did was drink! They were very smart about that: they had that south London, no-bullshit attitude, with a real work ethic. They didn't drink before they went onstage. None of that bollocks. When you come offstage, you can hammer it, but not before that. Not like the record company staff: back then, all the record companies used to do cocaine. If they went back to doing drugs, we'd be fucking laughing, because they'd be more liberal with their money. Put that in the book!

Luke We drank a lot, but I didn't smoke spliffs because I could never quite get it right. Either I'd feel nothing or I'd pass out, rather than getting that nice buzz that some people got.

Andy I think we captured all that on the record: that was the whole point. It was 60 per cent laughing, 20 per cent drinking, 20 per cent work. You're trying to make the environment uplifting. It's got to be special for you. Don't forget, 25 years ago, if you had a deal with EMI, it was kudos. Nowadays, if you say you've got a record deal, people say, "Really? Be careful…"

Left: Andy Taylor, along with a random stage invader, joins Thunder onstage for the climax of the Toilet Tour at the Opera On The Green in Shepherds Bush, London, in June 1989. Danny's rolled-up jeans and Snake's high-up bass are just the beginning of the comedy in this picture.

Danny While we were recording 'Dirty Love', Taylor suggested that we needed some tambourine at the end of the song. We asked Harry to do it, so he went into the studio with a tambourine, where we could see him on a TV screen. He couldn't see us, though. He waved this tambourine around for eight and a half minutes, because that's how long 'Dirty Love' was before the end faded out, and while he was doing it the big house rang up and told us it was dinner time. So the engineer recorded himself saying, "That's very good, Harry – just one more time" and set it on a loop.

We went to dinner and Harry was in there for an hour, playing the tambourine, just sitting there on his own with headphones. He was getting worried, because he wasn't being told why he had to keep doing repeated takes, and as the drummer he was supposed to have a good sense of rhythm. So he played harder, faster, slower... anything he could. Eventually he decided he'd had enough and went upstairs to the control room. When he found it empty, he realised what had happened and set off for the big house. He found us there finishing our dinner, and was not overly chuffed. I think "Bastards!" was the word he used. We pissed ourselves laughing. Another time, we bought an enormous fish head from the market and served it to him on a deli platter. He hates any kind of fish, so when he saw it he was almost sick.

Andy No one had really heard Danny do Danny before that; no one had really heard Luke do Luke. Luke can fucking blow any rock guitar player away – Slash, any of them. He's an incredibly skilled lead guitar player, but no one had really heard that. I was like, "What the fuck?"

Ben Linford Manor had two studios, so we booked them both for *Backstreet Symphony*. They were separated by 300 yards of parkland. The owner, who happened to be Harry Maloney – one of the managers after White Noize all those years ago – had to get British Telecom in to lay cables to link the two studios. The poor recording assistant became a seriously good long-distance runner by the end of the album.

Danny Luke is just about as objective as you can be for someone who creates music. He's very good at knowing when the right take is, and saying, "This is as good as it gets today." When you consider he writes the music, that's bloody hard to do. I don't think I'd be as objective as that.

Andy Don't forget, I was in a pop band, so I had lots of rock that I needed to get out of my system. I knew exactly how it felt to be in the wrong box. So the first Thunder album wasn't a task, because they were well rehearsed and they knew how to do things properly. They had great structure in their backing vocals and they can sing them live. They sit down and do that thing that makes you a good band.

Harry We'd all learned from the mistakes we'd made in Terraplane. This time, we wanted to be in a band that didn't fucking care. We looked at the Guns N' Roses model and played that album in the studio when we were recording the first album. I thought we were better than GN'R, with better songs, although they had a great attitude – which is what it was all about at that time.

Andy We really went through the process of doing the drums in a room where you can hear the boom, and Mike Fraser is God when it comes to getting guitar sounds. All the way, we wanted to push it and push it again. If you listen to Led Zeppelin's records, they pushed every fucking element of the sonics of the song, although you can't do that unless the band has the ability. But if they do, like Thunder have, then you as the producer, plus the engineer, can push them as hard as they can go in terms of a rock'n'roll sound.

It's not just about whether you can play a song: it's about, how far can we take the song? What are we trying to capture? And do we all agree that this is what it should sound like? They had the experience of Terraplane, so they weren't naive about the studio. They knew their technique. You didn't have to tell Danny how to use the microphone; he already knew. That motherfucker is so on it when he sings. I'd worked with Rod Stewart, Robert Plant and Robert Palmer, all those guys, and they're all like that. They go one, two, three, do the take, and say "Next!" It's great when you're producing guys like that, because if you

don't get the vocals in three takes, it dies; because it takes vocal chops to hit the notes. Don't forget, it was all done to tape: no Auto-Tune or any of that bollocks. It was men at work!

The wife of the maintenance guy at the studio where we did the first album turned out to be an old singer who I used to have in a covers band when I was 16. It was weird. So we threw them out of the maintenance department and turned it into 'Harry's Bar'. When you make your first album, if you don't fucking enjoy it, you're not going to get a second chance, so making that little bar was our way of saying, "Once the work is done, let's get fucking wasted." It gave us a little bit of motivation to get the recording done, then get dinner out of the way, and then get down to the bar.

Harry Andy was great at managing us: he knew whether he should get me pissed and relaxed, or just loosened up after a couple of drinks. He was very good for us and a fantastic laugh. We did a ridiculous amount of partying.

Andy I think I'm the only guy who ever made Harry lose his temper. I'm a lighter thief, and Harry was a proper 40-a-day man in those days and I kept nicking his lighter. What he didn't realise was that I wanted to wind him up so he would bang the shit out of the drums. As a result, it's a classic drumming album. That little fucker really banged it out, which was good, because he's such a nice guy – perhaps too nice! The drummer has to be an animal on an album like that, and Harry is very, very consistent on the drums, from studio to stage.

One important lesson which I'd learned was never to let anyone from the label in the studio. Never, ever, ever. I don't know why those people think they should be there. It's like putting a hooker on a building site: it's just going to cause a load of needless distraction. The artist will be in full flow, and then some wanker will come in and say the wrong thing and it kills the guy's confidence for six or seven days. It was incredibly arrogant of us, on the one hand, but you have to hold the line. I remember when we first let EMI listen to the album. They said, "The guitar's on one side." I told him, "Have you never listened to a fucking AC/DC record?"

So there we were. We'd signed a metal band to a British label, when no one else was doing it. The label couldn't come in the studio; we just fucked off and did it. Only when we had rough mixes at the end did we let the label hear it. I thought I did a fucking sterling job of creating an environment where no one would interfere.

When we were mixing the first Thunder album at AIR Studios, George Martin put his head around the door and said, "Hello Andy!" I knew him from the old Duran days, of course, because we were signed to his label, Parlophone. He asked, "What are you up to?" and I said, "I'm doing this rock band, George, called Thunder." "Very good, Andy!" I was blown away. Bryan Adams came in too. A lot of people heard how good this record was, while we were recording it. The buzz on it before we released it was fucking amazing. We were breaking a band: creating a whole new universe of rock! How many people get to do that?

Danny It really started to go mad at this point. We had to fly to America to shoot a video for the first single, 'She's So Fine', and then we did a full tour of the UK and Ireland, the Static Discharge tour. This included a couple of nights supporting Aerosmith in Birmingham. They hadn't played in the UK for years, and they'd had a big comeback album, so it was a real coup to get the slot. Our agent Rod MacSween had come up trumps. It felt like things were definitely moving.

Above:: With Aerosmith at the NEC in Birmingham in 1989. For reasons unknown, Steven Tyler held Harry's head and sang, "I wish I had a water melon"...
Right: The photo shoot for the cover of *Backstreet Symphony*. The record company reckoned the sleeve wouldn't work without a picture of the whole band on it, but we knew better.

Mark Those two dates were really important for Thunder. They showed that we were really starting to achieve things.

Snake We played a show in Shepherd's Bush, and on a chalk board outside someone had written 'Tonight – Thuder!' without the 'n'. Mick Wall will tell you a

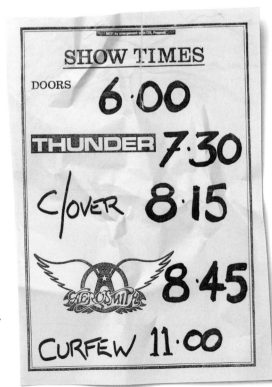

story about the Baggott Inn in Dublin on November 8, 1989, because he was writing about it for *Kerrang!*

Mick I was better known than Thunder were in Dublin at the time, because my Sky TV show, *Monsters Of Rock*, was popular over there. So when we got to the venue, the Baggott Inn, the punters were all buying me drinks while Thunder played. Danny invited me up to sing the encore, which I did, but I was so pissed that I fell on my face and knocked all the drums over. That was the end of the gig. I was very apologetic, but they were very relaxed about it and said it was no big deal.

Danny I'd completely forgotten about that. Silly Mick.

Luke We shot a video for 'Dirty Love' in December and the single peaked at number 32. To say we were blown away was an understatement. We were on our way. Then, we set off on a UK tour again and the album came out in March 1990. It made number 21!

Mark An example of Thunder's take-no-prisoners attitude is the album artwork for *Backstreet Symphony*: the front cover is a picture of Harry, a tramp and a woman in the doorway.

Luke Once we had the album title I thought about how we could interpret it in visual terms, and I got my mum to knock up a quick sketch of the street scene. It ended up being reproduced almost exactly by Andy Earle, the photographer.

Mark All the record company marketing people said, "You can't have a debut LP without a picture of the band on the front." The band put their foot down and said no. They liked the concept and they said they wanted to stick with it, the great thing being that they were able to say that in such a way that they didn't piss everybody off. People wanted to work with Thunder because they liked them as people.

BACKSTREET SYMPHONY

SONG BY SONG BY LUKE MORLEY

She's So Fine

The first song I wrote with Andy Taylor, and very much a statement of intent – which is why it was placed first on the album. A blueprint of what was to become typically Thunder.

Dirty Love

An important tune for us in so many ways. It was our one and only hit in the USA; it's been covered by a Canadian disco diva and the French megastar Johnny Hallyday; it was our first Top 40 song in the UK – and after 26 years we still close the show with it most nights.

Don't Wait For Me

A bluesy ballad with big dynamics that quotes many of our early influences: Purple, Zeppelin and Free in particular. It was always a big live tune on our early tours.

Higher Ground

This song uses the theme of getting away from a dead-end town to bigger and better things as a metaphor for how I was feeling about achieving something as a musician. It has a very uplifting chorus, which would explain why it's been another long-running tune in our live show.

Until My Dying Day

Another tune written with Andy Taylor. I had the acoustic section which makes up the first two minutes but couldn't work out what to do next. I played it to Andy and he instinctively picked up his guitar and went 'da-na-na, da-na-na' and we were off to the races.

Backstreet Symphony

This was the last song written for the album, and it came along at a very good time as we didn't have an album title until then! The intro riff is unashamedly stolen from 'Wichita Lineman' and the lyrical concept is a twist on Roberta Flack's 'Killing Me Softly'. She hears a young guy playing guitar and singing in a club (I believe it was Don McLean) and is drawn into his performance. Cunningly, the character in 'Backstreet' is a guy, and it's a girl singing in a club.

Love Walked In

When I came up with this idea I wasn't at all sure about it. I played it to Andy and he told me I would be insane not to put it on the album. I suppose he was right!

Englishman On Holiday

We've trotted off to Ibiza and the Canaries on more than one occasion for lads' holidays, and this song is a result of that experience. I'm glad I did it, but I wouldn't want to do it now...

Girl's Going Out Of Her Head

Sometimes, as a songwriter, things happen to you that are so bizarre you just have to turn them into a song. I've seen the young lady in question since, and she swears it was only a starter pistol!

Gimme Some Lovin'

During the recording of the album we came to the conclusion that we were probably a song short, so we spent an evening drinking too much and jamming through a few classic tunes. Andy sat in the control room listening, and when some time later we stumbled across this tune he cleverly asked us to try it again. I believe that the resulting take was the one we used. A moment of pure drunken spontaneity.

Distant Thunder

Another useful song in that it gave us our name! A fun, uptempo romp to close the album.

Danny In April 1990 we went back to the States to do two shows for the American media, one in the Cat Club in New York and another at the Roxy in LA. We'd signed to EMI in the UK and wanted to meet their US counterparts at Capitol, who we assumed would want to release *Backstreet Symphony* over there. Wrong again.

Mark Malcolm spent a lot of time working with the international department of the record company, with some successes and some failures. Unfortunately we had a major problem with Capitol, EMI's American label. It was all pretty grim.

Malcolm Before we even signed to EMI in the UK, I went to the American record company to be sure that they were behind us, because that was a key part of the deal. They paid for me to fly over to LA and I had a good meeting with their A&R head Tom Whalley, so I went back

to the UK and we did the deal, signing to EMI for the world. Between then and the album release, Whalley either left or was fired, and they brought in Hale Milgram, a suave, debonair chap who came to the Los Angeles show – which was stormingly good. Me and my American business partner Larry Mazer were there. Milgram went into the dressing room, shook everybody's hands and said, "Great show, great show!" and then came out into the corridor and said to Larry, "Sorry, I don't like it" and left. I said to Larry, "Find us another deal, because they're not going to put the record out."

Mick Capitol in America were notorious at the time for not supporting acts signed to EMI in the UK.

Malcolm I said to Howard Jones, our lawyer, "What are we going to do?" and he said, "See if you can find someone else to license it from Capitol and we'll try and

crack a deal." Larry went off to talk to people. Meanwhile, I was getting pressure from the band every day – "What's happening? What's happening?" – and I didn't have anything to tell them.

Snake We supported Heart for our first European dates in April 1990. At one of the shows our soundman was off sick and couldn't do the gig, so the American soundman did it instead – and when I stood onstage and played my bass, I could feel it coming through the PA system for the first time ever. The bass had been there before, of course, but it was much more mid-rangey, with far less bottom end than I wanted. I could hear it bouncing off the back wall, and I could see Malcolm telling the guy to turn it down!

Malcolm I can honestly say I never once told a soundman to turn the bass down.

Ben The Heart tour was such fun to do and our first real taste of touring abroad and playing in arenas. We spent many a drunken night with the girls from Heart, singing around the piano in hotel bars, usually until the early hours of the morning. Fair play to them, as they had a full show to do the next day and we were only doing 45 minutes. We ended up playing at Wembley Arena, which felt a bit like commuting to work as we were playing three nights. On the last night they asked us to get up to play Led Zeppelin's 'Rock And Roll' with them. Danny and Ann Wilson got into a singing contest at the end of the song: you can guess who won.

Luke The spring of 1990 was an exciting time for us. The 'Backstreet Symphony' single went in at number 25, we shot videos in America for 'Gimme Some Lovin'', played *Top Of The Pops* and did more European dates, this time with Love/Hate.

Malcolm I was at a Love/Hate show when I got a call from Larry Mazer, probably on one of those huge early mobile phones. Larry told me that John Kalodner, the A&R chief at Geffen, was a fan of Thunder. Geffen's three biggest artists at the time were huge rock bands – Whitesnake, Guns N' Roses and Aerosmith – and of course we had played with Aerosmith in Birmingham. Apparently their guitarist Joe Perry had been saying to Kalodner that Thunder were a great band. David Coverdale of Whitesnake had been in Kalodner's ear about us too. And then Axl Rose of Guns N' Roses must have heard us on the radio, because Kalodner told me Axl was a fan as well!

Above: Us with various execs from Capitol Records after a showcase at the legendary Roxy on Sunset Strip, LA. They said, "We love you guys!" and a week later we were off the label.
Left: Picture disc of the 'Backstreet Symphony' single.

Luke While Malcolm was sorting out the American deal, we were confirmed to open the Donington Festival in August 1990, where Whitesnake were headlining. We couldn't believe it.

Danny We did some warm-up shows in the week running up to Donington. After our new tour bus driver left the air conditioning on, my voice went during the first show at Buckley Tivoli. It was terrible. I could barely speak, let alone sing. None of us could believe the timing. Roger drove me back to London to see a Harley Street doctor after the awful warm-up show for Poison at Rock City in Nottingham. My voice was completely shot, and I remember crying and apologising to the punters for

Above: In the limo, or Co-Op funeral car as it actually was, about to set off to Donington 1990. Why aren't we smiling? Because we're terrified.
Right: Climbing the stairs to the stage at Donington, about to play the show that changed everything for Thunder.
Overleaf: Thunderbirds are go. Danny, Luke, Snake, Ben and Harry hang out with some of their fans (and the Thunderbirds) before the gig.

being shit. They cried too – it was a bit surreal, now I think back. I saw the doctor the next day and was given a steroid jab with instructions not to speak for a minimum of three days, and definitely no singing until the day of the show. It meant I couldn't do the soundcheck or hang out with the rest of the band the night before. The biggest day of my life was three days away and I had no idea if I was going to be able to sing. Bugger.

Snake Danny literally couldn't speak. He would open his mouth and nothing would come out. It made me realise how vulnerable you are as a rock band, because the vocals are so important. But he saw some specialists and got into the habit of using steam baths, and got through it like a professional. We had to have a smoke-free room for him, because we all smoked back then, especially Harry. I'd be lying in bed at night and I'd hear Harry wake up and light a cigarette in the middle of the night.

Roger Searle On the day, the management told me they wanted limousines for the band, so I went to the local funeral parlour, asked them to take the flowers out of the

back of four limos and hired them! I'd prearranged for a police officer to come out and escort them to the venue: they couldn't believe it when that happened.

Snake We were caught in traffic on the way to Donington, so these police outriders came to our rescue. At that point I really felt we'd arrived. It was like being in The Rolling Stones in the Seventies! But when we got there, we had to climb all the way up this gantry to the stage, and I'm not big on heights so I was crapping myself, especially because I thought we were going to get buckets of piss thrown at us as the opening band.

Harry That was squeaky-bum time. I had serious stage fright that day. I still get it now, although I don't think it's a bad thing. It shows I care. Once you've got the first two songs out of the way, it goes away. The audience were with us from the moment we started, as opposed to the debacle at Reading in 1987.

Luke I was very nervous. It was the size of the crowd that got me: 80,000 people!

Ben We were terrified that Danny wouldn't be able to sing. We did the soundcheck without him. I remember walking out onto the stage and looking out at the field where the punters would be standing. It was completely empty, and I knew that next time I walked out there it would be full of people – and we might not have a singer. That didn't help calm my nerves.

Harry We were all worried about Danny, but a doctor gave him a jab and the first note that came out was fantastic. I still remember the relief and elation I felt at that moment. It was a brilliant gig.

Snake There were Thunder flags everywhere. It felt as if we were spearheading the New New Wave of British Heavy Metal.

Mark We were all on a knife-edge because of Danny's voice. I went to the mixing desk and stood next to our sound engineer, and after he got through the first or second song, I knew he'd be fine because they were only playing 30 or 40 minutes. They went down a storm, because momentum had been building through the first few tours.

Danny It was terrifying stepping onto the stage. No warm-up, no soundcheck, no idea. There were rumours flying around that we wouldn't show up, because we'd cancelled the last warm-up show at the Marquee. Luckily the jab had worked and the voice was all there when I opened up my chops. The sense of relief for all of us was enormous. I'm sure that's most of the reason why we had such a good gig. It was a triumph, and things kicked right off for us as a result, but it could easily have been a disaster.

Snake I'd never been on an outside stage like that, and the sound was incredible. It was like listening to the CD. We were like kids in a candy store: it was an incredible feeling. One of the greatest moments of our lives, I'm sure. You would never get bored of doing gigs like that.

Ben As you looked out from the stage you couldn't see where the crowd stopped: they seemed to go on forever. It was one of the most memorable scenes I've ever encountered.

Malcolm John Kalodner was on Aerosmith's bus at Donington, listening to Thunder's set being broadcast live on Radio 1. Joe Perry told him, "See? I told you Thunder were great."

Andy Thunder did really, incredibly well in a very short space of time. Within nine months of their debut album coming out, they were first on the bill at fucking Donington. They wanted to get it right on their own terms, and maybe I had the wherewithal to get that front out of them. I remember being in the studio in London the day they played that festival, and Radio 1 were playing it, and I was sitting there thinking, "Fuck me! Fifteen months ago they were doing demos!"

Left: The look of disbelief on Danny's face says it all.
Above: Donington 1990 again: the only photo *Q* magazine ever published of Thunder. One of the photographers shouted, "Come on girls, get 'em out!" and the 'Thunderbirds' duly obliged. Oh well, if you must…

1990–1992

THE FELLOWS ENJOY THE FRUITS OF STARDOM TO THE MAXIMUM, BEFORE GRUNGE ARRIVES AND FUCKS EVERYTHING UP AGAIN.

Malcolm I expected Thunder to be successful. I knew that if we were clever about it, we could end up on the top of the pile. We all had an unshakeable belief that it was going to work. There were a number of key moments: one was when 'Dirty Love' made the Top 40, and the second was Donington. I was standing by the side of the stage with Nick Gatfield of EMI and we could see all the way to the back of the crowd of 80,000 people. They all had their hands in the air and Gatfield turned to me and said, "See that? That's a gold record." And he was right. Very shortly afterwards, *Backstreet Symphony* went gold.

As soon as it took off, we put all sorts of plans into place. We got the Thunderbirds thing going, which was where we hired five models in skimpy outfits to hand out flyers. It was very tacky but also very funny. At one photo call they got their tits out, and that was the only photograph of Thunder that *Q* magazine ever ran. That photo haunted us for years, because it positioned Thunder indelibly in a way that was particularly unhelpful. It was great for getting coverage, but it took years to escape the cheeky Cockney chappie image that it implied. Luke loathes all that stuff, but Danny doesn't mind so much because he is actually a cheeky Cockney chappie.

Not long afterwards, we signed a deal with Geffen for America. It was an incredibly complex negotiation, but eventually the record was licensed to them. It took weeks to sort out. John Kalodner was a funny little man, but he loved Thunder right to the end, even through the difficult times which were coming up.

Mick Kalodner told me that the reason he signed Thunder was because Axl Rose came to him and said, "This is my favourite new band." Malcolm told me that in the first meeting he had with Kalodner, Kalodner told him that Thunder would never even have crossed his radar if it hadn't been for Axl. He also said that the videos sucked and that Geffen would have to redo all of them.

> **KALODNER TOLD ME THAT THE REASON HE SIGNED THUNDER WAS BECAUSE AXL ROSE CAME TO HIM AND SAID, "THIS IS MY FAVOURITE NEW BAND."**

Snake When we went to America the first time, we were on Capitol Records, until they decided that they weren't really interested in us and we moved to Geffen. I met a girl over there and I didn't come back to the UK. I was effectively living in Los Angeles, which I loved. Luke would come over occasionally and we'd go out and have a blast. It was a fantastic time: we went out and did the Sunset Strip many, many times. The Whiskey, the Rainbow... what more do you need?

As I was living in LA, I'd go into the office at Geffen and help out. There was a thing called Dial MTV at the time, where the most requested video by phone would be a featured record that week. So I'd be the guy who made the phone calls to make 'Love Walked In', or whatever, the video of the week. That was a big deal back then. Everybody lived by radio airplay to boost record sales. I also did a few radio interviews, which was always funny because they always asked me about the song lyrics. As Luke wrote all the lyrics, all I could say was, "Well, what I *think* he meant was..." I did a couple of phone-ins too, and other weird stuff.

Mick Snake used to come over to my place in LA on his Harley. He was quite agitated, saying, "Thunder aren't doing anything. We're just sitting around!"

Right: "All aboard!" The good ship Thunder of course. What were we thinking?

Snake We did the *Backstreet Symphony* Tour Part 2 in the autumn of 1990, which went through Europe and ended up at the Hammersmith Odeon in London. Just before those gigs, we played the Radio 1 Weekend of Music at Wembley Arena in January 1991: the first day was indie, the second hip-hop and the third rock, and they only sold out the third day, which really gave us a boost. Bear in mind that Radio 1 never played any fucking rock back then. It was us, The Quireboys and Ozzy Osbourne, and the fans turned out in their masses. We played 'Backstreet Symphony' and stopped, and the crowd were making more and more noise. We just stood there, speechless, waiting for the applause to stop – but it didn't. It just kept going. That was one in the eye for the Whitney Houston fans, I thought. I knew we were on our way at that point. For me, that was a very important moment.

Harry When we walked onstage to play 'Backstreet Symphony', the audience just clapped us for five minutes. It was incredible.

Mark From having 200 or 300 punters on the earlier UK tour dates, suddenly we were up to 900 or 1,000. I remember one show in Sheffield which was absolutely crammed; I thought, "Something's starting to happen here."

Mick Every night was like an orgy on that tour. Every single night! In that situation, obviously the ideal scenario would be to take your bird up to your room, but sometimes that wasn't possible – and so they would all shag in the same room.

Danny Not everyone, and not in the same room. The very idea is disgusting, Michael...

Left: Danny in his natural habitat on stage. Nice pout.
Overleaf: A very proud moment and a great reason to celebrate at Hammermith Odeon as *Backsteet Symphony* goes silver.

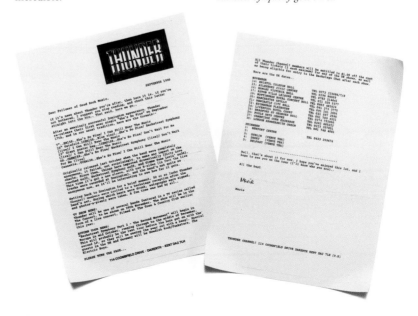

Harry In the spring of 1991 we went to America to do some promo. It was my first time there and I loved it. I didn't want to come home. The band were flying at the time, we were being treated like lords. John Kalodner appeared in the video for 'Dirty Love': there's me and him on the drums, and he's got JK shaved into his hair because I had my initials shaved into mine. Pamela Anderson is in that video too – it was before she got famous with *Baywatch*. Kalodner was an interesting fellow. He thought he was a rock star, which I suppose he was. He really liked me for some reason: he said I was the comedian of the band, but we're all comedians in this band. I suppose it was a talking point, that the band had a 'special' drummer.

Ben I had a real moment on arrival in LA. The record company sent a stretch limo to the airport, which Malcolm and I got into. There was a load of free booze in the back so we started drinking it. Then the driver switched on the radio, and what song was playing? 'Dirty Love'! I assumed the driver had put a cassette into the car stereo, but he told me it was on the radio. So there I was, quaffing champagne in the back of a limo, and the very first song I heard on the radio in LA was one of ours. How did I get to that point from Lewisham? It doesn't get better than that!

Malcolm 'Dirty Love' was all over US radio. I was at the Rainbow with Danny and Luke, and this bloke came in who we recognised. It was Axl Rose, with Erin Everly, who he was married to at the time.

Luke I got up to go for a piss and, on the way back from the loo, I noticed Axl sitting in one of the booths. As we'd actually

agreed the deal with Geffen that day and had had a couple of beers to celebrate, I walked up to his table with the intention of saying, "Thank you for helping to get us signed." I thought he was going to jump up and punch me when I first approached the

table, but as soon as I mentioned which band I was in, his whole demeanour changed. He stood up and we shook hands. I remember this vividly, because he had unbelievably small hands and such a deep voice compared to his singing voice! I then told him we'd love to buy him a drink, and they joined us at our table later on.

Malcolm It was the most surreal evening. Axl and Erin came over and sat with us. It was bizarre: even though he was sitting there next to his wife, a different girl would come over every couple of minutes and throw a bit of paper with her number on it on the table. He told Luke that he and Erin

had once had a fight and he had settled it by playing 'Love Walked In' to her. He also said that our CD was the only one in his car. We didn't think he was serious, but at the end of the evening his valet pulled up in Axl's BMW and 'Dirty Love' was playing. He said, "See?" and drove off.

Ben We travelled a lot that year. Thunder played gigs in Scandinavia and did a festival in Iceland. It was here that we discovered that the entire audience was drunk: strong beer had been legalised only a couple of years previously and they were obviously making up for lost time. We also played the Milton Keynes Bowl with ZZ Top and Bryan Adams, and then Danny and Luke went to Japan to do press.

Harry Bryan Adams was a very nice man, and so were ZZ Top. Americans understood what we were trying to do. It never got ordinary playing those huge gigs. I remember standing with Luke by the side of the stage, watching Bryan Adams singing '(Everything I Do) I Do It For You', which hadn't been released yet, and I said, "That's shit. It'll never hit the charts," and it was number one for 13 weeks, which shows what I know.

Danny In the summer of 1991, we were confirmed to do a massive US tour with David Lee Roth and Cinderella, with us opening. We'd shipped all our gear, and we were very excited, but the week before, Larry Mazer, our US manager and Malcolm's partner, called and told us to unpack. He said the tour was selling really badly and would almost certainly be cancelled after a week. His words were, "If you do this, you'll be like the house band on the Titanic." We were completely gutted.

Above: No pain but plenty of gain with the exclusive Thunder self adhesive Tattoo set!
Right: Our first photo session for Geffen in 1991.

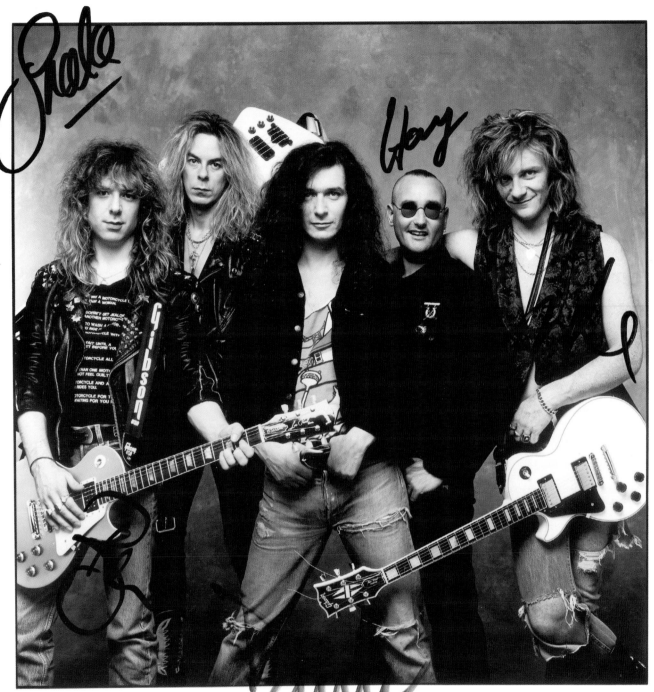

Ben Matthews   Snake   Danny Bowes   Harry James   Luke Morley

GEFFEN

Photo Credit: Glen LaFerman

© 1991 The David Geffen Company/Permission to reproduce limited to editorial uses in newspapers and other regularly published periodicals and television news programming.

Luke In September we had to go over to the States to make a video for Geffen for 'Love Walked In'. We worked out that the easiest way to do it was to get a tour bus to pick us up in LA, drive up the Pacific coast to the first gig in Vancouver, and then drive across Canada for a series of shows which we called the Drink Canada Dry tour, after the old Dean Martin joke. After going right over the continent, we did some shows on the eastern seaboard. Then we flew back to LA and played a show in San Diego, one in Orange County and then a party for *RIP* magazine. It was the first time I ever got a sense of the scale of America. That was the entire extent of our American touring, pretty much.

Mark Malcolm was the tour manager for the first Drink Canada Dry tour, and unfortunately he was totally the wrong guy for that job: tour managing is not what he does. He thinks in terms of the big picture rather than in terms of detail. At one point he got fined when they were crossing the Canadian border, because Malcolm had got the info from the merchandising man and it was wrong, so when customs checked the merch, Thunder had more than it said on the form. Because he was in charge, he got fined.

Malcolm Tour managing in Canada was very difficult. Snake was taking a lot of drugs and being a complete arse.

Snake I was very unhappy with the way things were going, and I got out of my head to try and cope with it.

Luke Malcolm's not a tour manager, and it was a very bad idea to get him to do it. It's all about living in each other's pockets, and Malcolm's not good at that – as indeed most people aren't.

Roger I worked with The Who from 1967 to 1976 – their best years, you might say! – so, as I always used to tell Thunder, there ain't nothing you can do which will cause me any concern. They were always well behaved. There were the usual tour shenanigans, but nothing seriously out of order. I don't recall any hotel rooms being trashed or anything like that: they were very civilised. They chased a few girls, that's for sure.

Harry Roger's catchphrase is "That'll be a lot of paperwork"... I had a bit of an interesting encounter at some point on that first Canadian tour. I met an attractive young lady at the gig and we went back to my hotel room for an evening of robust fun. In the middle of the night I got

up, feeling dehydrated as I'd been pretty pissed, and gulped down a glass of water that was standing by the bathroom sink before collapsing back into the bed alongside my companion.

The next day she woke me up, saying, "Have you seen a glass of water anywhere?" And I said, "What? That one in the bathroom? I drank it in the night." She went utterly ballistic and said, "You drank my eyes! You drank my fucking eyes!" It turned out she'd put her contact lenses in the glass overnight. I still wonder how she drove home that morning. Anyway, the lenses reappeared a couple of days later, as you might expect, but I didn't think she'd want them back at that point.

Malcolm The head of radio at Geffen decided that he wanted to release 'Until My Dying Day' as the second single, so they edited it for radio and butchered it, basically. So by the time we released 'Love Walked In' it was the autumn of 1991, and times had changed, because Metallica had released their 'Black Album', Guns N' Roses had released, *Use Your Illusions*, and, most importantly, Nirvana had released *Nevermind*. Grunge had arrived, and that was that. That was the point at which Thunder were finished in America.

> **GRUNGE HAD ARRIVED, AND THAT WAS THAT. THAT WAS THE POINT AT WHICH THUNDER WERE FINISHED IN AMERICA.**

Left: Harry praying for this photo shoot to be over, so we can get to the pub.
Above: Backstage with actor Christopher Guest, better known as Nigel Tufnel of Spinal Tap, at *RIP* Magazine's party at the Palace in Hollywood in September 1991. The other band sharing the dressing room was Pearl Jam. We were, of course, much more impressed by the Tap!

Harry I remember sitting in my flat and thinking, "We're off to America to support Dave Lee Roth, I'd better pack," and then the phone ringing to say that the tour had gone tits up in America because of the arrival of the new grunge scene. They thought mainstream rock bands like us wouldn't sell any tickets, and that we shouldn't bother coming.

It was unbelievable after all that work. We had Kalodner behind us, we had 'Dirty Love' on MTV; we thought it was going to be fine. It was disappointing – very disappointing. We'd built ourselves up for this tour for months, maybe years. We felt as if the carpet had been pulled from under us. But we don't do negativity: you can't affect us, because we believe in ourselves and we know we're going to do something else. We were unlucky there: it was bad timing.

Talking of bad timing, a certain event comes to mind from December that year when we were in Japan, the day after playing a New Year's Eve gig. I had a terrible hangover, because we'd drunk sake and lager and red wine, which is not a good combination. I was so ill, I couldn't even shut my suitcase – I had to ring the hotel reception to get somebody to help me. I went down and got into the van, and Luke gave me the plastic bag from the sandwich he was eating. Somebody gave me some orange juice, which I drank, but it came straight back up into the bag.

I got to the bullet-train station and there were Thunder fans there. Some guy asked me for an autograph, so I told him he'd have to hold my bag of puke. So he held it while I signed his CD and then gave it back to me. I chucked it in a nearby bin, but as the doors opened for the bullet train, the lovely lady stepped out and said, "Welcome" and I threw up all over her. Obviously everybody was laughing. Poor woman. She said, "Don't worry, it's OK," so I sat down, had a quick cigarette and went to sleep.

Snake I felt that Malcolm had fucked up Thunder's career. I really held him to blame for that. We were scheduled to tour the USA with Dave Lee Roth on a multi-band bill, but it was cancelled. I was expecting to fly from LA to Cedar Rapids to meet the rest of the band and then head out on a 30-date tour. But suddenly the tour was off. Malcolm came out to the States and he and Larry Mazer had a meeting with John Kalodner, Ed Rosenblatt and Robert Smith, the guys who basically ruled Geffen.

The meeting probably started well, but, as I understand it, they started whining about problems in the industry and how they'd made their money back on 'Love Walked In' and so on. As Mazer explained it to me later, Malcolm completely fucking lost his rag and unleashed a tirade of abuse at them. So that meeting ended, and Smith – the money man at Geffen – later phoned Mazer and told him that Thunder wouldn't get a red cent out of him.

Malcolm First of all, I never once had a meeting at which Ed, Robert and John were all present. That's not how Geffen operated. You always met these guys one-on-one. I was in the UK when that tour was called off – and it's true that I flew out to LA shortly thereafter and met with all three of these guys, but I met them individually. Each meeting was just two people – me and either Ed, Robert or John. Mazer wasn't even in California: he was at home in Philly at the time.

John Kalodner, who was our A&R rep, was as keen as we were to get things back on track, since the prevailing winds in the industry – and the label – were working as much against him as they were against us. Remember that John was closely associated with the Whitesnake, Aerosmith and indeed Thunder side of Geffen, which was on the wane, whereas Robert was very much the Nirvana guy, who were obviously the hottest thing in the States at the time. Robert was the VP of marketing – not the money man, that was David Berman – and hated Thunder, who he insisted on calling a hair band, from the get-go. He had told me as much in our first meeting a few months earlier.

The way it actually went down was I first met with John to strategise. He explained that I needed to get Robert on side, but that he was doubtful if he could be persuaded since Robert disliked the band so much and had been looking for any excuse to withdraw marketing support. He suggested that I talk to Ed, who was the president of the company, first – so I did.

Ed and I had a very civil meeting at which he explained that the Nirvana thing had changed everything, and that since AOR radio stations were moving to a new rock format in their droves, it was very unlikely that Geffen would be able to do much more with Thunder, but that John was still right behind us – and if Robert could be brought on side, he was fine with it.

Then I met with Robert, and he refused point-blank to help. His attitude was, "It's over." So many people had done so much work to get us to that position, and he was utterly dismissive. It's true that I got angry, but it's ridiculous to say that I unleashed a torrent of abuse. It was a difficult and fractious business meeting, with a guy who thoroughly disliked the band's music, but no more than that.

Afterwards, Robert did indeed call Larry in Philly to say that he wouldn't be supporting any touring activity, but he had made that decision long before I met with him. Larry then phoned me to tell me Robert had phoned him: he was as pissed off about Robert's attitude as I was. It is important to remember that the only people present in those meetings – and who actually know first-hand what went down – were Ed, John, Robert and me.

Luke Obviously, the one glaring omission from our CVs is America, but circumstances dictated that. I don't think there was anything we could have done about that. Grunge came at the wrong time and we were swept aside. We should have gone out there and toured on our own anyway, but hindsight is always 20/20.

Mark Exactly the same thing happened in the mid-Seventies in the UK, with punk. In 1977, all that journalists wanted to talk about with rock bands was punk. It was the same with grunge, at least in America. All the programming changed because plaid shirts and Pearl Jam were suddenly cool.

Malcolm We had a lot of radio support for the first single in America in some places, but none at all in others. Overnight, the majority of the radio stations changed their format to modern rock.

Luke We had bigger things to worry about, anyway. We were scheduled to record the second Thunder album in February 1992. We'd arranged to call it *Laughing On Judgement Day* and we had an amazing cover handmade by Storm Thorgerson of Hipgnosis, who had done all those amazing Pink Floyd LP sleeves in the Seventies.

Snake There's a couple of brilliant songs on there, although I'm not sure if people raved about it as much as they did about the first album. The studio we used had the biggest control room in Europe, apparently. It was in a beautiful barn.

Harry Andy Taylor was asked to produce again, but he had a lot of other things on his mind at the time: he spent a lot of time on the phone to his other business interests, and we felt that his mind wasn't quite on the job. He produced half of it, and Luke finished it. I think Andy was disappointed, but he understood. It's a fantastic record, and turned out really good.

Snake Andy was on the phone a lot, in a little antechamber off the main room.

Ben I recall a very drunken moment with Andy one evening on that album. He said to me, with a glass of whisky in his hand, "You've got my job." I said, "Sorry, what?" and he replied, "You've got my job – I wanted to be the other guitar player in Thunder." Although he and I worked happily on many other projects together later on, I always wondered if this might have been an issue.

Andy They had their American management by then and it was a much more complex album. Also, Mike Fraser couldn't come in and engineer, and for me that was difficult

Above: Harry and Luke as highly convincing ninjas with our old friend Tsuneo Omori on a Japanese promotional trip for *Laughing On Judgement Day* in 1992.
Right: The late, great Storm Thorgerson's brilliantly scary artwork for *Laughing On Judgement Day*.

because we'd been such a team on the first album. The songs were more refined too, so we did it in a different way.

Harry During the recording of the second album, we nicknamed Andy 'Gazza' because he's a Geordie and Paul Gascoigne was all over the TV at the time. In return, he called me 'Hazza', and over time it spread to the rest of the band, with Danny becoming 'Daz', Luke becoming 'Luz' and Ben becoming 'Bez'. We still sign our emails that way today. It's tragic, I know.

Malcolm Thunder's attitude served us well, no question. I was always able to negotiate from a position of strength, because they would always back me. If I told them, "I think this is a shit deal," they'd say, "Fine, let's do something else." That happened on a number of occasions.

Luke In May 1992 I got a call from our publisher saying that the French pop star Johnny Hallyday had recorded a cover version of 'Dirty Love' and wanted to buy the band dinner. I was in Portugal at the time, on holiday with Harry, so we got on a plane and flew to Paris. It was bizarre. I didn't have much understanding of how famous Johnny was. He was like a French, drug-addled Cliff Richard, if that makes sense. We turned up at this very swish Parisian restaurant, and he walked in an hour late and people started clapping as he walked in. He asked us to play on his album, and we played a gig with him in Switzerland the following year, although the audience didn't have a clue who we were. It was completely weird.

Mick I thought the single 'Low Life In High Places' from *Laughing On Judgement Day* was a genuine classic, even though by 1992 you had bands like Nirvana and Pearl Jam coming out and undermining their relevance.

Harry In the summer of 1992 we went over to do promo in Japan, although this time I didn't get quite so drunk, and then we toured in South America with Iron Maiden, which was a hell of an eye-opener.

Rod Smallwood Iron Maiden and Thunder were both on EMI, but because I was travelling a lot with Maiden I didn't actually hear of Thunder until *Backstreet Symphony* won Album Cover of the Year in *Kerrang!* That was our preserve – we thought, "Who are these scallywags taking over our position?" I thought it was a fantastic record with some great songs on it. I met the manager, Malcolm McKenzie, and we became pretty matey, and we still are. The band are a fun-loving bunch of guys. Danny's got a terrific voice and they write great songs. Luke, Ben, Snake and Harry were always pretty riotous.

They wanted to tour with us in South America and Malcolm thought it would be a good market for them, and I said, "The thing is, Malcolm, we're going to sell these gigs out: we can't pay you or anything," and he said, "No, I just want the exposure." So we played stadiums, and a bit of golf along the way, and we've been friends ever since. We were happy to have them along because they were such a good band. We all had a fucking good time.

Harry Those shows were great. We played golf with Maiden – they were better than us.

Ben I wasn't convinced about the food on that tour. We all went to a barbecue put on by the promoter, where they cooked every part of the animal. I pointed at a particularly interesting piece of meat and asked what it was. "Pene de toro," answered the chef, which doesn't need translating – or eating, for that matter.

Luke We were playing Donington in 1992, which Maiden were headlining, and we always got on well with them and their management, and there was an EMI conference going on in Rio, so it suited us to do the tour for various reasons. We thought it would be a great warm-up for Donington and it was fascinating to see how big they are in that part of the world. The rabid nature of the fans was pretty disturbing.

Snake I recall Maiden's bassist Steve Harris asking us to sing the chorus of 'Run To The Hills' with them, but their singer Bruce Dickinson apparently didn't like it, and so the rest of Thunder left the stage. I stuck stubbornly to the microphone, though – I think I may have had a few beers – and so Steve and one of the guitar players tried to push me off the front of the stage. I wasn't about to be thrown into the audience, so I pushed back through them, and was confronted by Bruce, who tried to give me a bear hug. I grabbed him round the neck and we fell over.

The band kept playing while we were wrestling, with legs everywhere. He couldn't move and neither could I, so we were shouting to each other, "Fucking let me go!", but neither of us would. At one point I raised my fist and said, "Let me go or I'm going to punch you," and as I said that I saw Malcolm by the side of the stage, looking at me and going, "Noooooo!" In the end we separated. I'd love to know if it was ever caught on video. I have a feeling it was filmed.

A few years later I met Bruce at an event and he said, "Bloody hell, Snake! I haven't seen you since we were rolling about onstage in South America. You were a lot stronger than I thought you were!"

Right and overleaf: Donington in 1992. We had a blast again. How could we not? We were on top of the world. The only thing was, the world was about to change direction...

Malcolm That tour was a lot of fun, but I'm not sure it helped us very much. It cost about £35,000 to do it. Rod told me to try and get EMI International to recoup the tour support out of South American sales, but of course they wouldn't.

Luke I don't know if we were the right band to tour with Maiden, to be honest! I think the fans wanted a band who were quite a bit heavier than we were.

Malcolm At one gig in Montevideo in Uruguay, people were throwing gravel at the band, which was slightly alarming.

Luke That was a very ugly incident. It was at a disused Victorian railway station and the promoter had built a makeshift wall around the site. There was a colossal number of people there, and five minutes before we were due to go on our roadie was getting a massive electric shock every time he tried to plug my guitar in, and then somebody else got thrown off the rig when he tried to climb it. Eventually they got the PA earthed and we went on.

The atmosphere was horrible, which is unusual for Thunder because we're used to going on and finding a friendly vibe. The stage had three ego ramps that reached out into the crowd, so when it came to the first guitar solo I trotted off down one of them. In my peripheral vision I could see this kid looking really malevolently at me, and he cleared his throat and gobbed at me. The spit landed right on my hand and he was like, "Yeah!" I went back to my roadie and asked him to clean it off, and then carried on. After a while things started to get thrown at us: nothing too sinister at first, just bits of fruit and the odd plastic bottle. I got hit by a plimsoll at one point.

Then, as the sun was going down, I started hearing all these pings around me: they'd started throwing coins, which are fucking dangerous, and you can't see them coming. The south-east London spirit kicked in a bit then: we thought, "You cunts!" and finished the set. The promoter, who looked like Don Johnson, came over and said, "They fucking love you!" – and I wondered what audiences did if they *didn't* like you.

> **AT ONE GIG IN MONTEVIDEO IN URUGUAY, PEOPLE WERE THROWING GRAVEL AT THE BAND, WHICH WAS SLIGHTLY ALARMING.**

We went into our dressing rooms and we could hear Maiden begin their set. Then suddenly all the music stopped and our tour manager, Roger Searle, came into our dressing room, saying, "I think we'd better get out of here fairly quickly." Maiden had gone onstage and the same thing had happened with the audience throwing coins, so Bruce had told them to stop or Maiden wouldn't play. The coins kept coming, so Maiden walked off. Roger packed us into the minibus and we took off.

Maiden did go back onstage and finished their set, but it was all very strange because our audiences are normally pretty friendly. There was one weird moment when we were playing a gig in St Austell in Cornwall and we were doing the intro of 'Until My Dying Day', which Danny was singing with his eyes shut. Suddenly he heard someone say, "Hello Danny" right next to his face. A punter had walked onstage, right past our security and all the way up to Danny onstage. It was funny as fuck.

Danny Funny for you maybe. I nearly jumped out of my skin!

We were invited to play *Top Of The Pops* to perform 'Low Life In High Places', which was released as a single in August 1992, and, to be honest, for a rock band to play that show is like pulling teeth. They don't want you to play live, because they couldn't handle that as it's a bit noisy. They wanted the singer to sing live but the band had to mime, which is a bit unfair and the song is an absolute bastard to sing. It really is. The second half, for a singer, is like being attacked in the knackers with a pair of bolt cutters. After running through it a few times, my voice was shot and I started to lose the will to live.

These kids in the audience were looking at us, thinking, "Who the fuck is this band?", and we didn't really care either. Eventually the director told us that it was time to record the actual take for real, and an old bloke called Reg – or Colin, perhaps – came in, wearing a brown technician's coat: typical BBC chap. He introduced himself as a BBC special effects specialist and said, "I understand that at two minutes 22 seconds, this song goes from very quiet to very loud. At that exact moment I will push a button and one of 20 bombs will go off in the studio, and you will be rock gods." I thanked him with a certain amount of trepidation, as the BBC are not known for being good at rock'n'roll.

So we did the song and, when we got to the loud bit, the bombs went off – but what felt like about 10 minutes after the correct moment. Afterwards Reg/Colin asked how it was, and we told him the bombs had gone off too late. The idea was that the bombs needed to go off when Harry brought his sticks down on the cymbals. So Reg/Colin said, "Don't worry, I've still got 19 bombs left. I've got it now." So we did it again, and again, and again... but he kept getting it wrong. We could hear the director yelling at Reg/Colin every time.

Finally we got down to the very last bomb: it had to be right this time. But this time he exploded the bomb way too early! He ran towards me, all expectantly, wanting to hear if it had gone OK – and none of us wanted to tell him that he'd got it even more wrong, so I said, "It was perfect, Reg (or Colin)." He looked genuinely pleased and said, "I told you I wouldn't let you down!"

Luke *Laughing On Judgement Day* went into the UK charts at number two, only beaten by Kylie Minogue's *Greatest Hits*! Who needed America anyway?

Ben That said, Kylie had to resort to a TV ad campaign to do it – that's cheating, in my book.

Left: A photo shoot on the set of the 'Low Life In High Places' video in 1992.
Above: The 'Low Life In High Places' single and the limited edition 7" single of 'A Better Man', complete with 3D cover and glasses.

THUNDER LAUGHING ON JUDGEMENT DAY

AUGHING ON JUDGEMENT DAY

ONG BY SONG BY LUKE MORLEY

es It Feel Like Love

s is typical Thunder: a mid-tempo
over featuring a sexually frustrated
tagonist who is having no luck with his
ended conquest!

erybody Wants Her

ery poppy tune for us. I really enjoyed
g a brass section to bolster the chorus.
nehow it made the whole thing a bit
re R&B, in the old-fashioned sense.

w Life In High Places

nder get serious for the first time! An
ervation on how life can be very difficult
big cities for young people and other
ple's obliviousness to it all.

ughing On Judgement Day

out as philosophical as I ever get. I think
is trying to make the point that we're
here for long, so we have to enjoy it.

npty City

ent quite a bit of time in Los Angeles in
01 and 1992 and I found it completely
cinating in the way it has the ability to
p human beings of their dignity. If
're not very grounded, mentally strong
itterly ruthless, you won't last long there.

Today The World Stopped Turning

During the writing of this album I was
involved in a relationship that inspired a
good few of the tunes. This one must've
been written after I'd been dumped!

Long Way From Home

This is kind of the antidote to 'Higher
Ground' in that it examines the effect of
achieving a degree of success, particularly
on the people around you.

Fire To Ice

How drinking too much can spoil a
perfectly good relationship. Thankfully, not
a personal tune.

Feeding The Flame

Don't let the bastards grind you down! This
song is all about using the negative
comments of others to drive you on to
better things.

A Better Man

It sounds daft, but when I heard the demo
of this song, for the first time I knew I
could really write songs. It only took me
until I was 31! It also made me realise the
power transmitted through lyrics by real
feelings, as opposed to anything contrived.
It only took me 30 minutes to write – I
wish it was always that simple.

The Moment Of Truth

This was written by Ben, Danny and Harry.
All I did was the arrangement. Obviously,
the trauma of writing together was enough
to stop them doing it again! A shame, as
this is a good tune.

Flawed To Perfection

During my time 'hanging out' in LA I did a
lot of people-watching, and one evening I
was in a rock club on Santa Monica
Boulevard. I was inspired by one particular
girl who appeared on the dance floor at
regular intervals. Everything she was
wearing was ripped, but very carefully
ripped, if you know what I mean.

Like A Satellite

A very simple 'I'm really missing you' type
song. Heartfelt at the time, and still a
popular live tune.

Baby I'll Be Gone

Another tune written with Andy Taylor. As
I recall, he came up with the drum groove
and it reminded me a little bit of 'When
The Levee Breaks', so we attempted to get
some of that Delta vibe going, which
explains the slide guitar and harmonica.

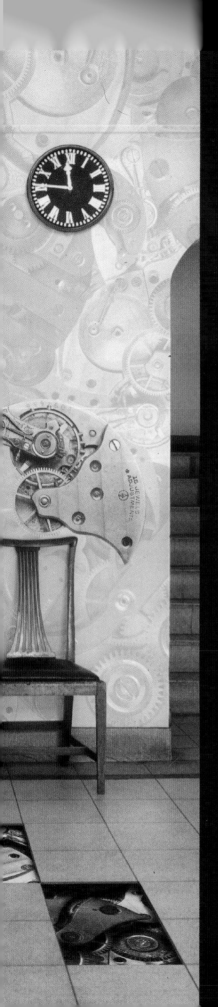

THUNDER

LAUGHING ON JUDGEMENT DAY

COMPACT DISC/CASSETTE/ * LTD. EDITION GATEFOLD DOUBLE ALBUM
14 Tracks, including the single **LOW LIFE IN HIGH PLACES**

* 15,000 Copies only, after which deleted   EMI

THE TOUR

MCP present

THUNDER

plus special guests

EDINBURGH PLAYHOUSE
Friday 2nd October
Available from venue box office, Tel: 031 557 2590
(Credit Cards accepted) and usual agents

ABERDEEN MUSIC HALL
Saturday 3rd October
Available from venue box office, Tel: 0224 641122
(Credit Cards accepted)

HULL CITY HALL
Monday 5th October
Available from venue box office, Tel: 0482 226655
(Credit Cards accepted) and usual agents,
(subject to booking fee)

SHEFFIELD CITY HALL
Tuesday 6th October
Available from venue box office, Tel: 0742 735295/6
(Credit Cards accepted)

ASTON VILLA LEISURE CENTRE
Wednesday 7th October
Available from venue box office, Tel: 021 328 5377
(Credit Cards accepted), Odeon Theatre,
Ticket Shop, Tempest Records, Birmingham;
MLM Wolverhampton; Poster Place Coventry
(subject to booking fee)

MANCHESTER APOLLO
Friday 9th October
Available from venue box office, Tel: 061 273 3775
(Credit Cards accepted), Piccadilly Box Office
and usual agents (subject to booking fee)

BRADFORD ST GEORGES HALL
Sunday 11th October
Available from venue box office, Tel: 0274 752000
(Credit Cards accepted) and usual agents,
subject to booking fee

HAMMERSMITH APOLLO THEATRE
Tuesday 13th &Wednesday 14th October
Available from venue box office, Tel: 081 741 4868
T&C Station, First Call, Ticketmaster, Premier, Stargreen
and Albermarle (subject to booking fee)

POOLE ARTS CENTRE
Saturday 17th October
Available from the box office, Tel: 0202 685222

NEWPORT CENTRE
Sunday 18th October
Available from venue box office, Tel: 0633 259676
(Credit Cards accepted), Our Price Bristol;
Spillers Records Cardiff;Booking Now Bath
(subject to booking fee)

PORTSMOUTH GUILDHALL
Monday 19th October
Available from the box office, Tel: 0705 824355

BRISTOL COLSTON HALL
Wednesday 21st October
Available rom the box office, Tel: 0272 223683
And all usual agents

NOTTINGHAM ROYAL CONCERT HALL
Thursday 22nd October
Available from venue box office, Tel: 0602 482626
Victoria Centre Box Office, Select-a-Disc and
Way Ahead Nottingham; Ainleys Leicester,
Way Ahead Lincoln & Derby and all usual agents
(subject to booking fee)

PLYMOUTH PAVILLIONS
Saturday 24th October
Available from venue box office, Tel: 0752 229922
(Credit Cards accepted)

ALL TICKETS £10.00

(Subject to a booking fee)

STOP PRESS: EXTRA DATE
BELFAST ULSTER HALL
Thursday 1st October
Tickets available from all usual agents & venue
Tickets £10/11 plus booking fee

Ben We were incredibly busy around this time. In late 1992 we did acoustic sets in London, Leicester and Manchester. I went to Canada, which was my first taste of being in an international priority band with EMI. It meant first-class air travel: I'd never turned left when boarding an aircraft before. Luke and Snake did press in America and Danny did Europe. We then started the Laughing All Over The World tour.

Danny Harry had been doing a short solo piece as the first part of the encore for live shows, usually just him and a guitar, and it was working well. On this particular tour, his song was 'Fly Me To The Moon', the old Sinatra classic – sorry, Frank! – and though it wasn't feasible on all the shows, we decided it would be fantastic if he actually flew when he did the song at the Hammersmith Odeon show, so we arranged it.

On the day, we got the 'Wire Man' in with his kit, and rehearsed it during the afternoon. We all had a go in the harness and flew about the stage like Peter Pan. It was great fun. The up, down, and back and forth flight was agreed, and the cue set for the beginning of the second verse of the first song in the encore. This was all set at 4 p.m., and the encore was set to take place around 10.30, so, with nothing else to do, Wire Man shot off. What we didn't know then was that, despite being certified and an expert in his job, he was also a raging alcoholic.

The encore came and we were all excited as Harry got strapped into his wire harness. We were on the other side of the stage in the wings, trying to stay out of sight, so when he looked across and mouthed the words, "He's pissed!". We didn't really understand what he meant, so we smiled and gave him a big thumbs up. Like a true pro, Harry realised there was no turning back, and of course he wanted his big moment, so he stepped out onto the stage, with his invisible wires and an acoustic guitar, and began the song. The audience loved it, none the wiser about what was to come.

The second verse arrived, and Harry sang it, braced for lift-off, but nothing happened. Wire Man was pissed out of his mind, having been in the pub for six hours, and missed his cue. Our tour manager was next to him, realised he'd missed it, and gave him a dig, shouting, "Up!" Wire Man reacted immediately – overreacted, actually – and gave his apparatus a sharp yank. Harry shot up into the air at about 500 mph, colliding with the lighting truss, then shot back down to earth at the same speed, hitting the deck way too hard. Then he went up again just as fast, then left, way past the safety curtain in the wings and into the wall, then right, into the other wall, then back into the middle.

> **HARRY SHOT UP INTO THE AIR AT ABOUT 500 MPH, COLLIDING WITH THE LIGHTING TRUSS, THEN SHOT BACK DOWN TO EARTH AT THE SAME SPEED, HITTING THE DECK WAY TOO HARD.**

There was a lot of "oof" and "ugh" as he collided with everything in his path – the floor, the truss and so on – but he didn't stop singing and playing the whole time. The audience was laughing so hard they had tears in their eyes, obviously thinking it was all arranged, and while we realised something was awry, I must confess we all laughed too.

When he finally came down to earth – with a bang – at the end of the song, the audience was going completely nuts as we walked on to embrace him, while Wire Man fumbled with the straps and struggled to remove the harness. Harry turned to me and said, "What went wrong?" I said, "Nothing, mate! Listen to the audience – we've got to put it in every night." He was not amused, and very bruised, but he had his big moment, and it was a triumph.

We never got him in a harness again.

Left: The *Laughing On Judgement Day* tour, 1992. Danny's first daughter was born (very conveniently) the night after the Aston Villa show. He got there in time for the birth, spent the day with the family, and then rejoined the tour in Manchester.
Right: Harry getting ready to fly. This sometimes led to disaster, but we laughed anyway.
Overleaf: We were unstoppable when we hit the stage. Young and full of passion, we took every venue by storm.

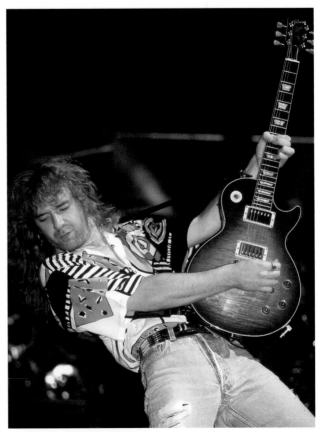

Harry In December we went to Japan again, which is when it all went tits up with Snake.

Roger At the first show in Japan, Danny injured his leg in the first song when he jumped off the drum riser.

Danny I did the rest of that show sitting on the drum riser, with a towel filled with ice on my knee, and a bottle of Scotch.

Harry Snake's a lovely fellow, and we're great friends now, but at the time he was being moody and argumentative, and it was bringing everybody down. I don't know if he was having problems at home or something, but there was a lot of negativity

coming from him. He also had a lot of opinions on how the band should go, and, with hindsight, maybe some of those opinions were right. He was getting exasperated by the fact that nobody was listening to him.

Roger Malcolm used to travel everywhere with the band, and I think Snake didn't like that. He wanted Malcolm to be at home taking care of business.

Malcolm If I could change one thing, it would be that I wouldn't have spent so much time on the road with them in the early days. It made my job harder in many ways. That said, I got a lot of marketing information from physically being there at the shows.

Ben I liked Snake, but he'd pissed everyone off. He was Jekyll and Hyde, that was the problem. When he was on form, he was brilliant – so funny. When he wasn't, he was really moody. He's still the only person in Thunder I've ever argued with. It sounds weird, but it was over a towel in Canada! Obviously, the bigger picture is that it wasn't about a towel; it was about being cooped up in a tour bus for hours on end with someone who was being very negative. Nobody else in the band had those moments, so we didn't understand why they were necessary. Perhaps it was in his nature to be a little bit self-destructive.

Harry Snake was a bit moody at times, it's true. Nobody's perfect, though, and if you didn't have characters around, life would be boring.

Snake It's totally accurate that I was up and down a lot. In fact, 'up and down' is an understatement. I wasn't depressed in the clinical sense, but the downs that I had were bordering on depression. I felt unable to say anything about the problems we were having because they were unwilling to listen to me and act upon what I was saying. I was caught between the devil and the deep blue sea, to coin a phrase, and I was deeply unhappy sometimes. Sometimes I'd sit there and be jolly; other times I'd sit there and say, "Oh for fuck's sake..." – especially when I was hungover. There was a bit of coke flying around as well, which made it worse. It was a miserable time.

Ross Halfin: When I first met Snake, I liked him, but as time passed he started saying things like, "Fucking Luke... fucking Danny... is this all about them?" whenever there was a photo shoot with those two in it. I'd say, "Come on, Snake, they're the leaders of the band. It's the same as Ozzy and Iommi, or Page and Plant, or Daltrey and Townshend." But he was resentful, and he'd say, "Why am I even fucking bothering? It's a waste of my time."

Snake No one likes to be treated like a cunt, and it seemed like a waste of time to arrive at a photo shoot and get ready to be photographed when it had already been decided that it would only be Luke and Danny in the picture. I had the mother of all arguments with Ross in Japan after a show on Harry's birthday, and I ended up chucking Harry's birthday cake at his head.

Ross Snake was sulking because the cover of *Kerrang!*, which I was shooting, wasn't a group shot: it was just Luke and Danny. When he went at me with the cake, he didn't just do it for fun: he did it nastily, shoving it as hard as he could at me, and making a point of aiming it at my camera.

Danny After the cake incident, there was a deathly silence. The Japanese label were deeply embarrassed to have witnessed it.

Snake If that was the worst that the label staff had seen from a rock band visiting Japan, then they need to get out more!

Danny This kind of confrontation is a very big deal in Japan, and it was clear to all that Snake had overstepped the mark. Once we'd laughed it off and they'd left, I retired to the non-smoking dressing room, and then Ross came in, wiping cake off his face and clothes. He was fuming, and muttered that if it hadn't been for us and the label, he would have chinned Snake. I told him not to hold back on my account.

Snake Bits of cake got on Ross' camera, which obviously pissed him off, and he wanted to start a fight, but Luke and Malcolm got in the middle of us and nothing happened. Later on that night, we went out and I sat with Benny and Harry, while Ross sat with Luke and Danny. I ended up having a massive row with Danny about all the problems we'd had in America. I blamed the band as much as I blamed Malcolm for all that stuff.

Ross Snake was trying to provoke me, saying, "You wanker... you wanker," until Luke told him to stop. At the final gig in Japan, Snake started on Danny about me, saying what a fucking cunt I was. Danny turned to him and said, "Ross isn't the cunt. *You're* the cunt, and at the end of this tour, you're done." That was how he got fired.

Danny Having hurt my knee jumping off the drum riser in the first song, I was in a lot of pain during the whole gig. I'd drunk nigh on a bottle of Scotch by the time we got to the club after the show was over. It was the last night of the tour and I was sitting in a booth, while the others came and went. When Snake and I got into the discussion at the table, it was with others initially, then just the two of us when it ended. He brought up the cake incident and I tried my best not to get into it, as I knew it would end up in a row. He wouldn't let it go, though, so I told him I thought he'd made himself look a tit in front of the label.

Eventually he said, "I guess I'll be getting chucked out of the band when we get home, then." He was saying it like he was joking, but he was fishing for a reaction. I thought, "Why not? You've asked," so I said, "You've done it to yourself." He looked a bit stunned, initially, then walked off and joined the others. They'd all been looking at us across the bar, expecting a punch-up. It didn't get that far, but there was a lot of quiet menace going on.

Snake Booze always leads you to say things that you wouldn't normally say, and it led to my downfall, if you like. But everyone drank in that band: Luke was as big a drinker as me. Thunder were a boozy, boozy band back then, and when you live in close proximity for all those tours, everything gets magnified.

Luke Snake is a really good bloke, but I don't think being in a touring band is for everybody. He'd get up in a black mood sometimes...

Snake Those moods were called hangovers!

Luke ...and none of the rest of us are like that. Occasionally people say things when they're in that kind of mood that don't get forgotten, unfortunately.

THUNDER LOSE THEIR SNAKE!

THUNDER, the stalwart UK Rockers who scooped the RAW Readers' Poll winning the 'Best UK Band' and 'Best Album Sleeve' categories as well as making a sizeable showing in the 'Best Band', 'Best Album', 'Best Live Show' and 'Best Promo Video' slots, have parted company with longstanding bass player Mark 'Snake' Luckhurst.

The five-piece of Luckhurst, drummer Gary 'H' James, guitarist/rhythm guitarist Ben Matthews and mainmen Danny Bowes (vocals) and Luke Morley (guitar) have maintained a consistent line-up since the ex-Terraplane duo of Bowes and Morley put the outfit together back in mid-'89 in deepest South London. The band then signed to EMI shortly afterwards to release their début LP 'Backstreet Symphony' (gold in the UK) and last year's highly successful 'Laughing On Judgement Day' opus.

The reason for the split seems to have been down to a clash of attitudes although the band had recently completed a successful tour of Japan. Thunder are currently seeking a new bass player to honour European touring commitments. More news on the situation as soon as the appropriate announcements are made.

The outfit also issue a new single, 'A Better man' on February 1 on EMI. It's taken from their 'Laughing ...' LP.

United we stand, divided we fall: Thunder's Luke Morley (left) and the now-departed bassist, Mark 'Snake' Luckhurst.

Danny Snake and I didn't speak again on the way back to the UK, and Luke fired him after Christmas. We didn't speak for years.

Ben We got back from Japan and decompressed for a couple of days. Snake called me at home first, as we were probably the closest. He asked me how everyone had reacted to the incident, and if a decision had been made. It was obvious he wanted to know about his future employment. I told him, "It doesn't look good. I think you're going to get fired." He was already

resigned to the fact and took it very calmly, all things considered.

Snake Luke rang me up and said, "We've all had a chat," and I thought, "That's nice. If only you'd included me!" And he said, "We've decided that you need to go." I didn't protest too much. After I put the phone down I felt a mixture of real disappointment, because I really loved all those guys and it was like leaving a family, but at the same time it was a relief.

Luke I get on much better with Snake now than I did then. I only ever had one argument with him when he was in the band, and I don't remember what it was about.

Snake I get on fine with all of the guys now. It all happened many years ago, after all. I played with Coverdale & Page and then Medicine Head after leaving Thunder. Since then I've been in the property development business. I saw Thunder a couple of years later, went backstage and said hello and it was all fine. In 2011 I played with Joe Elliott in his band Down'N'Outz, which was a lot of fun. People have asked me over the years if I'd play with Thunder again, and of course it would be a lot of fun to do – perhaps on an anniversary tour of the first or second album.

Danny We've always stayed friends with everyone who was in the band. If we've ever fallen out with anybody, it wasn't for very long. Life goes on, doesn't it?

1993–1995

RECORD COMPANY AND MANAGEMENT CHANGES PLAGUE THUNDER – AND MAJOR DEVELOPMENTS ARE ON THE HORIZON.

Malcolm So now we're in 1993, and we need a new bass player. And we found one, but not where we expected to find him.

Nick When Snake was fired, I auditioned for Thunder, and I got down to the last two candidates. It didn't happen, but I understood why it would have been difficult for them to have me back in the band.

Mikael 'Micke' Höglund My band, Great King Rat, split up at the end of 1992, which was a big setback for me personally, and I was quite down for a while. Then our guitarist told me that Thunder was looking for a new bass player, so I gave Malcolm a call and asked him what my chances were of getting the job. He told me that my chances were as good as anyone else's, and that I could come to the UK and audition if I paid for my flight myself.

I took the next flight over and met them at John Henry's rehearsal studio in London. I waited in the cafeteria and, as I was eating my lunch, I asked myself, "Why am I here? I must be crazy to think I can get this job in a British band, when there are so many bass players in this country," and I got ready to leave. But then Danny came up from the rehearsal room and said hi, so I went down and got ready to play.

Danny Mikael came to us from a Swedish band called Great King Rat,

which had had some success in their native land before disbanding. Malcolm put him forward for the audition, and I remember liking him immediately. He seemed quite nervous at the audition, but he put it all into the tunes when he played them, and he looked great.

Harry Micke's a wonderful man. He came along to the audition and played great. Typical Swede: he liked a drink.

Micke The next day Malcolm called me and said, "You must have made a good impression: you're down to the last three." I was happy with that. I assumed I'd go home to Sweden at that point, but then he called again and asked if I would go up to Rock City in Nottingham with them, where they were doing a personal appearance event.

Danny It was pretty obvious to us all that he was going to get the gig, so after a quick chat we decided to take him with us to Rock City in Nottingham to help us judge a wet T-shirt contest (remember, it was the Nineties). He got drunk while we did the judging, and in a spontaneous moment we dragged him out onstage and introduced him to the crowd as our new bass player. I honestly don't remember whose idea it was, but it felt right at the time. He joined the band, and it clicked immediately.

MICKE WAS A VIKING, AND DRANK LIKE ONE. EVERY NIGHT ON TOUR, HE DRANK UNTIL HE FELL OVER.

Micke It turned out that they just wanted to see what I was like when I was drunk! So while they were onstage, signing stuff, I was drinking in the dressing room. They came in and invited me to come and sit onstage with them and I said, "Sure." After a while Luke said, "You can consider yourself a member of the band now!" Obviously they did like me when I was drunk. So we headed to Canada for the second Drink Canada Dry tour, which had an appropriate name, I thought.

Danny Micke was a Viking, and drank like one. Every night on tour, he drank until he fell over. He used to take his clothes off and stand on the table, saying, "On behalf of the rhythm section, I would like to propose a toast!" People would be trying to stick things up his arse, but he was so pissed he didn't care.

Micke It was great. Being in a band like Thunder, playing at an international level, had been my goal for years, so I was over the moon. All the guys were cool to me and I was as happy as Larry. Playing in Stockholm was big for me, because it's my home town. In the UK, a few musicians were a bit unwelcoming, like "Why are you here, when there are lots of British bass players already?", but they were the minority.

1993 / 31164
© EMI RECORDS UK – PHOTOGRAPHER: JILL FURMANOVSKY

THUNDER

EMI
UNITED
KINGDOM

Ben I have to say, at first I wasn't sure about having a Swedish bass player join the band, because I couldn't see how it would work. Sometimes it's great to be wrong: Micke soon proved to be a great bandmate, although he had a particularly annoying habit of playing very loudly onstage. As I stood next to him, it usually fell to me to ask him to turn it down to a reasonable volume. He would turn to you with a smile on his face and say, "But it's my sound!" You couldn't help but smile and put up with it – he had that ability to get away with anything.

Danny Black Sabbath were Micke's favourite band and their bassist Geezer Butler was his absolute hero. Because of that, we used to torture him with jazz versions of Black Sabbath songs, just to get up his nose. We did it all the way through the band and he absolutely hated it.

Ben I think Micke's influence on Thunder is greater than people realise. His love of Geezer Butler and all things Sabbath was reflected in his playing and his songwriting contributions to *Behind Closed Doors*, giving it a darker and heavier feel. That, and the fact we can all swear in Swedish...

Micke My first UK gig was supporting Def Leppard in Sheffield, so I was understandably nervous, and I drank a lot – which I don't normally do before a gig. I didn't feel drunk because I was so nervous, but I only remember the first four bars of the first song, and then leaving the stage at the end. I felt sober at that point, but halfway to the dressing room it all kicked in and I was really drunk. I've listened to the gig since then and I played all right, fortunately.

Above: The first Jill Furmanovsky photo session with our new bassist, Mikael Hoglund, in London in 1993.

Danny Micke was with us for three years all told, and lived in my house when he was in the UK, which was most of the time. He was very funny, and we laughed a lot, especially when I found out he was not quite your typical Viking. It turned out he was scared of spiders – which we discovered while watching the film *Arachnophobia* on TV when he had to keep going outside to 'smoke' – and he's also scared of heights. Look at his expression on the cover of the 'Stand Up' CD single, which was shot high up on a coal belt at Battersea Power Station – he was shitting himself. Another time at the pictures, he kept grabbing my leg at the end of the James Bond film *GoldenEye* – you know the fight sequence at the end, when Pierce Brosnan is having the punch-up with Sean Bean on top of the giant radio telescope? I took the piss out of him relentlessly for days afterwards. Cruel, I know – but damn, Viking, ha!

Ben We were all playing golf on a day off on tour, and Luke was having a pretty lousy round, stuffing his ball into a lake on several occasions. Micke hit the perfect shot right onto the green, turned to Luke and said with a grin, "I love this game. How about you, Luke?" He knew exactly what he was doing, the little bugger!

Luke We hit the road again in 1993. As far as I recall, we played festivals in Switzerland and Holland before a show with Rod Stewart and Tina Turner in Germany. And we released a single, 'Like A Satellite', and we did a Danny & The Doo Wops tour as well.

Right: The legendary Danny & The Doo Wops, from left: Mojo Filter, Otis Blue, Eddie Spaghetti, Belmont Cyclone and Danny Ocean. They're great guys. We hope to meet them sometime.

Danny In April 1993, we were on tour in the south of Germany on a day off. It was the night before my birthday, so the booze flowed copiously in the bar. The barman was wearing a very strange wig – we couldn't take our eyes off it. Our tour manager Ross Duncan and I decided that someone should relieve the poor barman of his dodgy 'hair' as soon as possible, to help make him realise once and for all that baldness is something to be proud of. The demon alcohol plays a huge part in such decisions, as we all know, and so, to make it extra worthwhile, a bet was agreed, whereby Ross was to remove the wig and run out of the bar before me. If he managed it, I'd pay him £50.

When it happened, it was as if the whole world suddenly went into slow motion: the hand across the bar, the excruciating sound of the wig pulling away from the double-sided tape on the barman's head... Ross and I sprinted from the bar, but Ross caught his shoulder on a pillar as he ran, jolting his arm and causing the wig to fly out of his hand and land in the middle of the hotel lobby. We did a runner and one of the crew picked up the wig, but refused to do anything, so Ben came out and took it back to the barman.

Prior to that, the barman had asked Harry if he could help him. Harry just felt his head, sighed and said, "You've picked the wrong bloke, mate."

Sides aching, I eventually went back to the bar to see what had happened. The barman was naturally very upset and lectured me endlessly about how cruel I'd been. Then Ross came back too, and the barman tried to knife him.

Then the Danny & The Doo Wops tour came round, and of course Micke, as the bass player, was inducted on guitar, as Ricky Malmo.

> ## "
> ## WE ALL GREW PENCIL MOUSTACHES, AND PUT MASCARA ON THEM, PLUS BRYLCREEM FOR THE HAIR, AND TUXEDOS – EXCEPT FOR BEN, WHO HAD A PURPLE SHIRT AND A DOG COLLAR.
> ## "

Martin We did that Danny & The Doo Wops tour properly, with a tour bus and nice hotels and so on. I was living the dream! We went down a storm everywhere, except in Mold in North Wales: we'd been booked as Thunder, so all the bikers turned up expecting to hear heavy rock, and our first song was 'Buzz Buzz Buzz' by The Hollywood Flames. It was hardly rock'n'roll. I remember a beer bottle flying past my head and our security guy, a massive chap called Mick The Cat, moving through the audience, glaring at people. By the end of it the audience was on our side, though.

We were a good band, although we didn't take it too seriously: we had the 'Brockley Horns', for example, which was me and Danny playing kazoos. Embarrassingly, the record company got wind of us and asked if we could play their Christmas party in the West End, and they asked what backline and instruments we'd need – and when we got there, the stage was full of saxophones and trombones, hired that afternoon. We stood there playing kazoos, surrounded by all this brass.

Part of our rider was an altar cloth, a candle and a Bible for Ben, who came out a bit like a Southern Baptist preacher. He had this amazing bejewelled crucifix with flashing lights on it: it was really impressive. We all grew pencil moustaches, and put mascara on them, plus Brylcreem for the hair, and tuxedos – except for Ben, who had a purple shirt and a dog collar. One night, we arranged to meet by the lifts and go down to the lobby together. We were all there, pointing at each other's costumes and laughing, and when we got into the lift a load of genuine clergymen joined us. The whole lift went quiet – and Ben stood there, blessing them! As soon as they got out, we all collapsed in laughter.

Danny We're all going to hell. You know that, don't you.

Harry In May 1994 we started pre-production for our third record, *Behind Closed Doors*. I'm very proud of that album. Mike Fraser and Luke produced it; we recorded it in America.

Luke In 1994 the shock waves of grunge had died down a bit and we found ourselves still contracted to Geffen in the US. They released *Laughing On Judgement Day* but it had barely been noticed, and we'd done absolutely nothing in the way of promotion. As a last-ditch attempt to try and motivate Geffen, we decided we would go to the USA to make *Behind Closed Doors*, the theory being that if we involved John Kalodner, our American A&R man, in all the creative conversations, we might stand at least some chance of the label stepping up to the plate. I remember flying over to LA three or four times during the writing of the album to meet with Kalodner and get his input. In the end it made no difference, as Kalodner was about to follow Aerosmith to Sony Records, although I do remember him coming to Record Plant Studios for a playback when we'd finished the record. Without a hint of irony he said, "This is the best album I've ever made"! The album was never released over there, but we did at least have fun making it.

Micke The drums and bass were supposed to be recorded at Southern Track Studios in Atlanta, but our guitar tech was a big dope smoker and completely useless. When I asked him to set up my bass to make it as easy to play as possible, as you do when you start recording, he loosened the bolts that hold the neck to the body so that the strings and the fretboard were closer together! And because I was playing at the same time as Harry, I couldn't hear that I was playing out of tune, so we had to do the bass all over again in LA.

Ben We had great fun introducing the owner of Southern Track to English cuisine. We decided to make him a Sunday roast: beef was on the menu and Danny was head chef, along with Malcolm as his assistant. I had managed to find some Colman's English mustard and stuck it on the table.

The owner thought it was American mustard and liberally applied it to his food. By the time we finally scraped him off the ceiling and explained the difference, he'd lost all trust in our culinary expertise.

Harry When we were in LA, Prince was recording at the same studio, but we were instructed by the studio bosses not to look at him if we saw him. Did we obey that command? Fuck no! I was going out for a ciggie and he walked in with two huge bodyguards, and I said to him, "All right, mate? How you doing?" He looked at me as if to say, "How dare you talk to me?" He was a great artiste and songwriter, but nobody's going to tell me or the boys in the band, "Don't look at me." Absolutely fucking ridiculous!

Luke In 1994, when we were in the States making the third album, Andy Taylor and The Power Station were making their second album. For my 34th birthday, we were recording in the Valley and they were recording somewhere else in LA, so Andy's wife Tracey threw a party for me. It was the most surreal evening: OJ Simpson's freeway chase happened the night we played with King's X at the Palladium, and we went on late because we were watching it backstage.

Above: Grunge had arrived. It was time to take ourselves seriously... or maybe not!
Right: Welcome to band of leather.

Danny At the end of that year we released 'Stand Up' as a single, so we did *Top Of The Pops* again, and when we got there about 50 female Take That fans were there all with placards saying 'Robbie I love you', 'Marry me Gary' and so on, with their phone numbers written underneath. We thought it was hilarious. Our massive American people carrier had blacked-out windows, so they couldn't see inside, and they all started screaming, obviously thinking we were Take That. We opened our windows a little bit and waved at them, and they screamed even more because they could only see our waving hands, not our faces.

Afterwards, they were still there, so we did the waving act again and drove off laughing, thinking it was all so funny. But five minutes later we were on a dual carriageway and they were driving behind us in a load of tiny cars, all with girls hanging out of the sunroof, holding up these placards with their phone numbers on and screaming. I thought we should really phone one of them up, so I asked the other members of the band if they fancied impersonating one of Take That. There were no takers, so I did it.

When the girl picked up, the screaming coming down the phone was off the scale. After a minute this voice came down the line saying, "Hello, who's this?" and I said, "Hello, it's Mark Owen here." The rest of them were lying on the floor, pissing themselves with laughter at this point. So the girl shrieks, "Aaaagh!" down the phone at me. Eventually she calms down and we have a conversation, and I tell her all about what Take That were doing. I made it all up. This goes on for about 10 minutes and eventually I hang up.

Then I make another phone call to another one of them, and this time I was Gary Barlow. This goes on for 90 minutes until we've gone all the way to the other side of London. By then I've impersonated all of them! The silly girls were too busy screaming to notice my terrible accents.

> **OUR MASSIVE AMERICAN PEOPLE CARRIER HAD BLACKED-OUT WINDOWS, SO THEY COULDN'T SEE INSIDE, AND THEY ALL STARTED SCREAMING, OBVIOUSLY THINKING WE WERE TAKE THAT.**

We were about 10 minutes from Luke's place, and it suddenly occurred to me that these girls were still chasing us – and what was going to happen when we got there, climbed out of the car, and they realised we weren't Take That? They were going to kill us. I could just imagine the headlines: 'Thunder Killed By Girls'.

The only solution I could think of was to drive faster, so I told the driver to put his foot down. Off we went, faster and faster. Eventually we beat a set of lights and the girls got stuck there: we were jumping for joy. Finally we got to Luke's house, leaped out of the car, hid behind a wall and told the driver to get out of there. It turned out that he drove down to Brighton and they followed him all the way. Rock stars hiding behind walls to escape rabid girl fans: now there's an image to conjure with. Rock'n'roll, baby!

Luke And *Behind Closed Doors* went into the UK chart at number five!

Left: Never a man to do things by halves, Storm Thorgerson had this stained-glass window made for the *Behind Closed Doors* cover.
Above: Photos for the *Behind Closed Doors* album artwork. To this day no one knows who the people are...

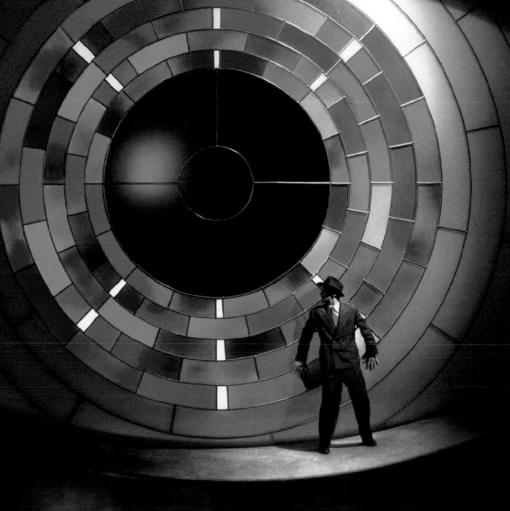

BEHIND CLOSED DOORS

SONG BY SONG BY LUKE MORLEY

Moth To The Flame
A strange song. The intro riff originally started out as a repeated phrase on the fade-out, but it was so hooky that it became the intro. This was written with Mikael and Andy Taylor, although I can't remember who wrote which part of the tune.

Fly On The Wall
Very funky for us! Lyrically it's about the intrusiveness of the press and their 'stop at nothing' approach to getting the dirt on whoever is newsworthy at the time.

I'll Be Waiting
This song is quite at odds with the rest of the album, in that it's shamelessly romantic. It's a tip of the hat to Hendrix and Santana.

River Of Pain
About loving someone too much and the consequences. Still a very popular tune, particularly in Japan for some reason.

Future Train
The strange Eastern riff I think came from Micke, Harry and Ben, and the lyrical mood was definitely influenced by what was going on in LA in 1994 when we were recording – Rodney King, the race riots, lootings, OJ Simpson and so on.

'Til The River Runs Dry
Looking back at this album, I think I was consciously trying to broaden the lyrical content in our tunes, but I'm really not sure where this came from. Domestic abuse isn't something you usually find in rock songs. Harry came up with the chord sequence and melody, and the lyric happened very naturally.

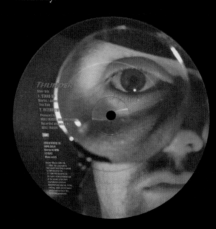

Stand Up
Harry came up with the riff and I took it from there. This is a very straight-ahead, rabble-rousing tune and great to play live.

Preaching From A Chair
While we were in the States in 1994 recording the album, grunge had really taken hold of the media. I read an interview with Soundgarden in which they moaned about being successful and how awful it all was, and it pissed me off to the extent that I felt compelled to write about it. There was a real cult of misery at the time; never smile, stand still onstage, moan about everything. No wonder we didn't fit!

Castles In The Sand
I guess we're all looking for the right relationship, or at least the one where there's not enough wrong to make you want to end it...

Too Scared To Live
Our A&R man at Geffen, John Kalodner, told me he thought this song was 'a piece of crap'. A week later he declared of the album that "This is the greatest record I've ever made," all without a hint of irony! In comparison with the general mood of the album, this is a bit of light relief.

Ball & Chain
A co-write with the rest of the band: they started it and I finished it. This became quite epic as a live tune, incorporating 'Nut Rocker', the theme to *Hawaii Five-0* and even Booker T's 'Soul Limbo' at one point: the latter is most famous for being the theme to the BBC's cricket coverage.

It Happened In This Town
As dark as we've ever got. A teenage girl was raped and murdered very close to my home in London and it moved me to write the lyric after Harry had come in with the initial idea.

Danny Having reached the conclusion that our deal with Geffen was dead, in late spring of 1995 we headed off to Europe again. We spent the best part of two months on the road there, in the UK and back to Europe. Then in the summer we were asked to do a series of outdoor shows supporting Bon Jovi in the UK, Holland and Scandinavia. The special guests on the UK shows were Van Halen, with Sammy Hagar on vocals.

Harry At one point Van Halen summoned us into their dressing room, and we wondered what the fuck was going on. We loved that band: their first two albums in particular. They said to us, "We've invited you in here to tell you off, because you're kicking our asses every night and we don't like it. Stop it now!" Of course, it was in very good humour. It was a huge compliment. But then, we are shit hot. We always believed in ourselves and we always will do. There are some bands who genuinely don't like us supporting them, because we're too good.

When we played Wembley with Bon Jovi, that was one of the best gigs we've ever done. The fans were right on the ball: from the front to the back, they were fantastic. I came away thinking, "My God, this is the best." The sound was amazing, we played amazing – and I remember noticing that Jon Bon Jovi had perfectly trimmed chest hair. It was fantastic. Jon Bon Jovi came up to me and Luke at the party afterwards and told us we'd been great. And we were great

– he was right. I remember my then wife standing there and saying, "My God, Jon Bon Jovi's just approached my husband." She was very impressed with that.

Danny We were about to get dropped by EMI, although Malcolm didn't seem to think that was the case. The moment EMI suggested a greatest hits album, my first thought was, "That means we're off the label. They're trying to get the money in before they heave us out of the door." So we went down to the Wool Hall Studio in Bath, which was then Van Morrison's studio, to do some extra tracks for the greatest hits album, which we knew was the death knell. Once again, Malcolm wasn't having it: he was convinced that it was going to be OK. We re-recorded a couple of songs and recorded a cover of 'In A Broken Dream' by Python Lee Jackson, which went on to do very well for us.

While we were down there, we were working with the producer Dave Bascombe, who had worked on the second album with us. It was good to see him again: Dave is a wise old sage. I remember me sitting there

and saying, "Here's the thing, boys: we've got a manager who doesn't really see what's coming, we're gonna get dropped by EMI and I think it's a good thing. We must owe them a million quid, and at our royalty rate we'll need a number one hit all around the world to recoup it. We'd have more chance of earning money from EMI if we all cut our hair, put chinos on and go to work in the marketing department."

They laughed, but I was serious. We had allowed the record company to build our brand by spending a lot of our money. They get their money back because they get the vast majority of revenue from every sale, so we were better off taking ourselves somewhere else and finding a new sponsor. EMI dropped us in the summer of 1995 and we fired the management around the same time.

Luke On July 27, 1995, we had the meeting with Malcolm that we all knew was coming. We had to seek new management if we were going to move forward.

Danny I'd completely lost faith in the manager. There had been key times previously when things had not gone as well as they could have done, and by Malcolm's reaction at those times it was obvious that he wasn't seeing things the way they were. Luke and Malcolm used to talk about artistic, creative, big-picture stuff, while I always looked at the details.

Mark Harris always did a good job – solid and focused on the nuts and bolts. There was no ego with Mark. I always got the feeling that he was unhappy with the way the company was going, while Malcolm was clinging on grimly.

Right: The serious, 'urban decay' shot that all bands had to do in the early Nineties.

Ben Mark is a glorious fellow. I always insist that he comes to stay with me when he's in England.

Danny Vicky McIvor, who was Malcolm and Mark's right-hand woman, had already told me that she wanted to leave before we fired them. I told her, "Go – and good luck. I'll never try and hold you back if you've got things that you want to do. We've had a great time, and you're lovely and I'll be sad to see you go, but you have to do your thing." I'm not particularly sentimental, but I do believe in loyalty and treating people well and all those truisms. I try to live that way. You won't find anybody who tells you I've crooked them out of money, or went back on a deal. But if people want to go, they should go.

Malcolm I knew something was up when I couldn't get Luke on the phone. In all the time I've known him, the only time I've been unable to reach him is when he's been about to fire me. So I knew something was going to happen. Then I had a conversation on the phone with Danny, where he was unusually brusque with me: he wanted me to do something to do with the greatest hits record they were releasing. I remember him shouting at me, "I want it done exactly like this. Not like that, like this!" which I thought was a bit odd.

Then I got a call saying that the band were coming in for a meeting at my office. I strongly suspected what was going to happen. They walked in with very grim faces and Luke was a bit pale. He was the one who did the talking. He said words to the effect of, "We've thought about this long and hard. It's one of the most difficult things we've ever had to do. You're fired." I didn't think there was much point listening to them explain why, so I thanked them and walked out.

Mark I was at that meeting with the band, and was sacked along with Malcolm. I didn't take it personally: it was a business decision, and I understood why they were making that decision, so I was aggravated about it for maybe a week, no longer than that. It was different for Malcolm, though, because he'd been friends with them for so long.

Harry I was disappointed to see Malcolm go, but also relieved. He'd put a lot of work into the band, but perhaps he'd lost the plot a little bit. Perhaps a few decisions – not major ones – had gone the wrong way, and Danny was getting pretty clued-up about management by this point. He's very bright and you could see the wheels turning. It was definitely time for us to seek new management.

Ben I was in the Maldives with my girlfriend when they fired Malcolm I think the others were a bit annoyed that I wasn't there. But I didn't give a fuck. I told them they should have done it two years before. Of course, Malcolm made a lot of good decisions for us over the years, but it was time to move on.

Malcolm It was personally hurtful, because I'd put so much into Thunder. I suppose we could have continued as music managers with other artists, but I was sickened by what had happened and thought, "Fuck this." I understood why they'd done it: they were cleaning house because things weren't going their way.

Danny I remember a summons to appear in court in New York arriving on my doormat one day. It was from our US merchandise company, and they were suing us for half a million dollars. We'd signed a lucrative merchandise deal a few years before, but the expected touring didn't

come to pass, so the merchandise company had been asking for their money back. Malcolm had been handling it all that time, and we had no idea how bad things had got.

Ben My problem with Malcolm was essentially that he managed Luke, and that there was a lot of fawning over Luke going on. Danny was aggressive enough to whip Malcolm into shape, and Malcolm was slightly fearful of Danny as a result. He didn't worry about me and the various bass players because we weren't important enough, and Harry was generally relaxed about things. I think this had played a large part in Snake's unhappiness. So, from my perspective, Malcolm managed the careers of Danny and Luke, which was not a problem because I trust them to make good decisions, and they always have. Their only mistake was not sacking Malcolm earlier.

Mick To me, Malcolm was the classic early-days manager – part mate, part fan – who assumed a role and did a pretty passable impression of it. Things happened so quickly that it went beyond his capabilities, and I think the major mistake that they made was that they didn't do what Def Leppard, Queensrÿche and Metallica had done, and leapfrog onto a major management company. I blame Thunder's relationship with Malcolm for their lack of global success. It wasn't Malcolm's fault – it was the band's fault for not moving on. He was very well-meaning and very hard-working. In fairness to him, he was doing his best, and he was thrust into it. He had a lot of balls to front it out.

Mark Malcolm decided he'd had enough of management and went off to become an executive at MTV; Vicky decided to carry on in management, but outside the music industry; and I decided that I would carry on managing Andy Taylor, who we were managing already. We were also working with The Power Station, who needed a second guitarist at the time, so Luke joined that band and I ended up managing him for that period of time as well.

Above: The 'River Of Pain' 12" picture disc.

1996–2000

IT'S GOOD NIGHT FROM US: PART 1.

Luke In 1996, Andy Taylor rang and asked if I'd like to play guitar in The Power Station, which I said I would as long as it fitted around what Thunder were doing. It did, so I did that for some of 1996 and into 1997. It was fantastic. I'm lucky in that I've only ever worked with really good singers, so working with Robert Palmer was amazing: he was a nice guy and a musicologist. He also liked to enjoy himself colossally: he went out as he would have wanted to, I think.

Ben I joined Luke and Andy for a bit of songwriting at his place in Spain, while Danny took care of business back home.

Danny I was setting up our label, which we called B Lucky, which was licensing the next album, *The Thrill Of It All*, to Castle Communications. Micke had told us that he was going to leave, so Luke played bass on the record.

Micke When I joined Thunder they were peaking, and it felt as if we lost a lot of momentum between that point and the release of *Behind Closed Doors*. Grunge had come along, too. I enjoyed being in the band, but they were going downhill a bit and they'd fired Malcolm. Those weren't the main reasons I left, though: the main reason for leaving was that my girlfriend was pregnant. I would do it all over again, though, if they asked me. I had a great time!

> ## WE WERE ALL VERY SAD INDEED WHEN MICKE DECIDED TO LEAVE. I HAVE REALLY GOOD MEMORIES OF HIM BEING IN THE BAND, AND WE STILL STAY IN TOUCH.

Ben We were all very sad indeed when Micke decided to leave. I have really good memories of him being in the band, and we still stay in touch.

Danny I was sad when Micke called to tell me he had to leave the band. We all were, but because of him being at my house so much, I felt like I'd lost my friend as well as a bandmate. I didn't see him again until Luke's 50th birthday bash, when he came over to London. We stayed up all night talking cobblers and drinking too much. Terrible hangover, but well worth it...

Luke We decided to make the album with me playing bass, as we didn't have any gigs coming up for a while and we didn't want to get a new bass player and then go straight into the studio. So we made the album, and then the misery of auditioning began again.

Danny We couldn't quite make one of the songs on *The Thrill Of It All* as good as we wanted, so I did the trick that always works – I went to Threshers, bought the entire shop and presented it to the band. I said, "Drink that, and we'll do the song again."

Ben We drank all the red wine that Threshers had, just on that one session. It was a shedload – and just as well, because we were all really fed up with that song. Pretty soon we were joking and laughing and pissing about. It's so easy recording with Thunder. I know through my previous recording experience of working with so many other musicians how much fun it is recording albums with this band.

Danny After a while we recorded a jazz version of 'War Pigs' that we'd used to annoy Micke with when he was in the band. About 30 seconds of it appears at the end of the record, ages after the official last track ends. We affectionately refer to it as 'The Moonlight Club'. It has no track number – a kind of secret track, if you will.

Left: Micke up to his thighs on the set of the video for "River Of Pain", in the swimming pool near QPR's football ground in London. He never did get used to the British weather, way too warm!

Above: And then there were four... The band come to terms with the departure of Micke and Danny's long locks.

115

Chris In the early Nineties I started working with Mark Shaw, formerly of Then Jerico, and through him I met Andy Taylor, forming Then Jerico[2]. An album and a fair amount of touring ensued, and a tenuous link to Thunder was established: I met Luke for the first time when he came to a Then Jerico[2] show in Birmingham. Mark's manager was always going on about how he was mates with Thunder's management, and how great they were, so I said, "Why not put me forward for an audition?" and he said, "Oh no, they're a league above. You'll never get a gig with them."

On October 28, 1996 I auditioned for Thunder. We had a lot of mutual friends and I'd done a couple of gigs with Harry at various times, so off to Terminal Studios in London I went. I'd never heard a single Thunder song before that audition: there's still a load of songs that I've never heard.

A few weeks previously, I'd auditioned for Gary Glitter. I didn't get the gig.

Harry I think I brought two or three bass players to that audition: I'm obviously the bass-player-finding drummer.

Chris I played 'I'll Be Waiting', 'Backstreet Symphony' and maybe 'Dirty Love' with them. It went well, but I didn't get the gig! They gave it to somebody else, who didn't work out, and then I auditioned again in November 1996 and got the gig.

Ben Chris is incredibly accomplished as a musician. He also has a great ear for mixing, so he took over that job from me when I was ill in 2014, and did a bloody good job of it too. And he does graphic design too – he's a bit of an all-rounder, that boy. Our very own Ian Botham.

Luke Chris auditioned last, and he was so much better than anybody else that he was the obvious choice. He was so good – everything that we'd been looking for in a bass player. I'm sure Snake and Micke won't mind me saying this, but I'm as good a bass player as they are – and it was nice to have someone in the band who was as fully rounded a bassist as Chris is, and who can play any style of music. He makes the band sound different and feel different; he meant that we could play songs that we couldn't play before he came along. Everything I've

recorded since, I've always asked him to play bass on it.

Chris My first gig with Thunder was at a secret gig at the King's Head in Fulham. I was blown away by the audience's reaction. To this day I've never seen a band that has a rapport with its fans like Thunder does. That was a real eye-opener for me. What happens at a Thunder show is unique. There's a lot of warmth and enthusiasm and a real party audience. I remember that Tony Thompson, the drummer from Chic, was there, which was amazing for me because I'm a big Chic fan.

Harry Chris is a very talented man and a great, great bass player. He's a great audio engineer and designs the T-shirts as well. It was great to have him on board for the release of *The Thrill Of It All* in 1997.

Left: Ascot, 1996 and television horse racing pundit John McCririck thought he was the 1000 to 1 outsider to become our new bass player. **Above:** Fortunately Chris had by far the best odds and joined the band in November.

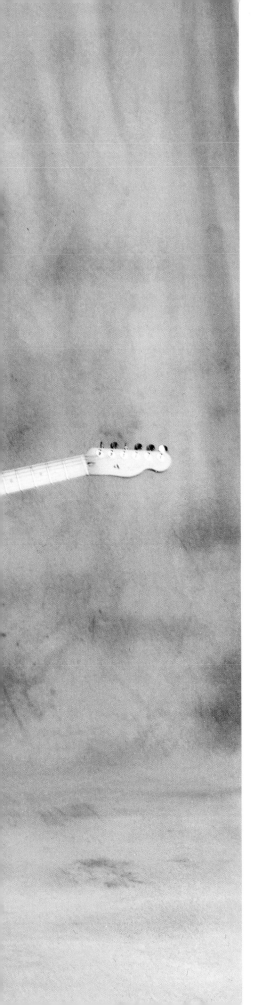

Danny Castle Communications released *The Thrill Of It All*, and if you know what I'm like, you'll love this story. Around this time my wife was pregnant with our son, but we didn't know that at the time: we weren't even trying for a third child. One day she went to see a spiritualist with her mother, basically just to keep her mother company. She came home and her eyes were like saucers, and she said to me, "You have to go and see this man." I said, "You've got to be joking," but she nagged me rotten for about three weeks so I made an appointment, just to shut her up.

So I went to see this guy, who was a slightly effeminate old boy called Robert Wood. Everything about his house was roses: roses in the garden, roses etched into his front door window, roses on the carpet, roses on the walls, cut glass roses in a display cabinet! He asked me in and offered me a cup of tea. We sat in the parlour and he said, "You didn't want to come here, did you?" and I said, "No. I don't believe in this stuff." But then, for the next hour, he proceeded to tell me things about myself. He didn't ask me any questions. And almost every single thing he told me was true.

I was deeply disturbed by this. These were things he couldn't *possibly* have known about me unless he was getting them from someone close to me. He knew about my relationships with my siblings; my relationship with my grandfather and my father; and very specific things such as a feeling of guilt which I had about the breakup of a relationship. He thought it was a relationship with a female, but actually it was about Malcolm. I did feel guilty about Malcolm I'd known him since I was 13 years old. I knew it had to be done, and I didn't shy away from the decision, but I didn't feel good about what I'd done to Malcolm, or to Mark for that matter.

It was really odd. I felt like someone had been in my head. The only thing he got wrong was that he said the name

Dougie was important to me somehow, but I didn't know anyone of that name and insisted that he must be wrong about that. He just shrugged. Six months later we signed to Castle Communications. The MD of the company? Dougie Dudgeon!

Luke When Malcolm went in 1995, we had a lawyer friend of ours called James Wyllie take care of us with his partner Steve Blackwell. He got us out of our first ever management contract with Robert Wace in the Eighties. He's been a friend for a long time. So he looked after us through our deal for *The Thrill Of It All* with Castle Communications.

Ben After that, a woman called Toni Medcalf managed us for a while. She'd worked at Mercury as a product manager with Bon Jovi and Def Leppard and was a friend of Luke's. She was ambitious and wanted to stop working for a record label and become a manager, so when she started working for Sanctuary, effectively we were a Sanctuary-managed act along with Iron Maiden and a load of other bands.

Luke We knew Toni socially and she was looking for a way to set up on her own, which is basically why we did it. We went into the Sanctuary deal with a degree of trepidation, because the scale of their operation meant that they have a lot of bands and a lot of departments, and we felt that we had established a team of people that we liked to work with. They had the way they wanted to work, too, and we were a little resistant to that. As much as we love Rod Smallwood and his business partner Andy Taylor – not our producer Andy Taylor, note! – who are great guys, the contract that they offered us was almost Dickensian. We knew it wasn't really going to work for us in the long term, but we needed somebody to take care of things.

Left: What a lovely pair of Telecasters! Our shy, introverted guitar players get back to nature. Never at any stage did anyone believe this was a good idea, yet it happened anyway.
Overleaf: Contact sheet from photo session with Phil Nicholls.

Danny Although Toni was officially managing us, I was the de facto manager from about 1997 onwards. She and I had a very full and frank discussion about what was right and what was wrong about the record and the release. Being signed to Castle was a bit of a culture shock. It was all amicable, and they were good people, but we didn't feel we were getting anywhere. The backdrop of the time wasn't helpful: it was very difficult to get written about or get any kind of reviews, and there was no internet yet.

I basically went into Castle and made them pull the release of *The Thrill Of It All*, and they were very unhappy about it, but it hadn't been set up properly. The problem was that they'd already spent quite a lot of money, and in my naivety I thought they would just spend it again later when it was released properly – but of course they didn't. When they came to release it the second time, the money wasn't there, so we kind of shot ourselves in the foot there. I still think it was the right thing to do, although I got labelled as the unmanageable artist. I don't want the band to make mistakes and spend their money badly, so when we got the chance we left the Castle deal and signed to Eagle.

There were definitely some benefits to having Rod and Andy on side while we were with Sanctuary. I told you about the court case in New York over the merchandise deal. I knew Rod and Andy had a relationship with the guy who ran the merchandise company, so I told Rod about the problem, and he had a word. I don't know what was said, but it got sorted out pretty quickly.

Luke Rod got us out of a very sticky situation with that merchandising deal. We'll be eternally grateful to him for that.

Danny We did the *Giving The Game Away* album with Toni and the double live album before that, both for Eagle. Luke and I conceived the idea that we would do a live and a studio album for them, so they would get some money back quickly. John Knowles, the MD at the time, loved the idea: we got on very well with him. The problems came later, against the backdrop of the times once again. We had loads of marketing ideas, none of which we thought were particularly expensive, but the record company always said, "We can't do that." We felt very frustrated once again by what we felt was a lack of commitment.

I remember we had a full-page advert in *Kerrang!*, back when they still wrote about us, and there were a couple of snidey comments that snuck in, like, "Oh, it's good old reliable Thunder, does anybody still care?" and so on. It didn't bother us because we knew that fashions come and go. We knew that if they loved us at one point, they'd turn on us later. Rock music is like the tide: it comes in and out.

When we were on EMI in the early days, we went to a conference and we sat there at the table with Martin Fry of ABC, who wanted to talk about football, and Robert Palmer, who was very drunk. EMF played their song 'Unbelievable' at the conference and we sat and watched them. I said to Palmer, "Jesus Christ! That's a hit, isn't it?"

and he said, "Yes it is, but I tell you what, the trick in this business is not having a hit, but staying around long enough to have another one." That was a pearl of wisdom, as I saw it: you have to weather the storms, because you are going to be in and out of favour – and as time goes by, his words keep coming back to me.

We knew in this post-grunge period that we could still sell tickets to the people who loved us, so we didn't need the media to do that. It just made it hard to get anything going on when we released new albums. Perhaps there would come a time when they changed their minds, but in the meantime it was like water off a duck's back. I had to have that conversation with the band the whole time, especially with Luke, because his songs are like his babies. He takes it personally, which is understandable when you've put so much into them.

Harry A video for the 'Love Worth Dying For' single was shot in January 1997, but it never saw the light of day, and it never will. They wanted me to jump up and down in Doc Martens boots and a fairy outfit. We went with it for some reason, rather than telling

them to fuck off. We made a few cock-ups of that kind with record companies, who were generally well-meaning but didn't really get Thunder.

Danny I caught pneumonia and laryngitis in Japan: not pleasant. We had to cancel six shows in the UK when we got back, but I got better after a couple of weeks. Then I had to have a knee operation a few months later, all while running the B Lucky label and managing the move to Eagle Records towards the end of 1997. At least we played with Kiss at festivals that summer, as well as getting the

live album recorded in November. That album made the Top 40 when it came out in February, so we were obviously doing some things right.

Chris My first tour with Thunder was in Japan, when Danny caught pneumonia. Later we came back to the UK, and I'll never forget, we were set up at Sheffield for the first show of the tour, and there were queues all round the block. Everything was set up and we were ready to do the soundcheck and Danny said, "I can't do it." He was very ill. So the tour got pushed back and we tagged the cancelled shows on the end. The vibe at those gigs was great, though.

Danny *The Thrill Of It All* felt like a different album when it came out in February. Luke stretched out in a more soulful, funky direction. He's never been the kind of writer who wants to make the same album over and over again, and the band don't want to do that either. The goal is to move your fans along with you without losing them, so we wouldn't make a reggae album, for example – although now I think of it, why not? Ha ha!

Left: It's in the can and that's where it's going to stay. The film canister containing the unreleased video for 'Love Worth Dying For'.

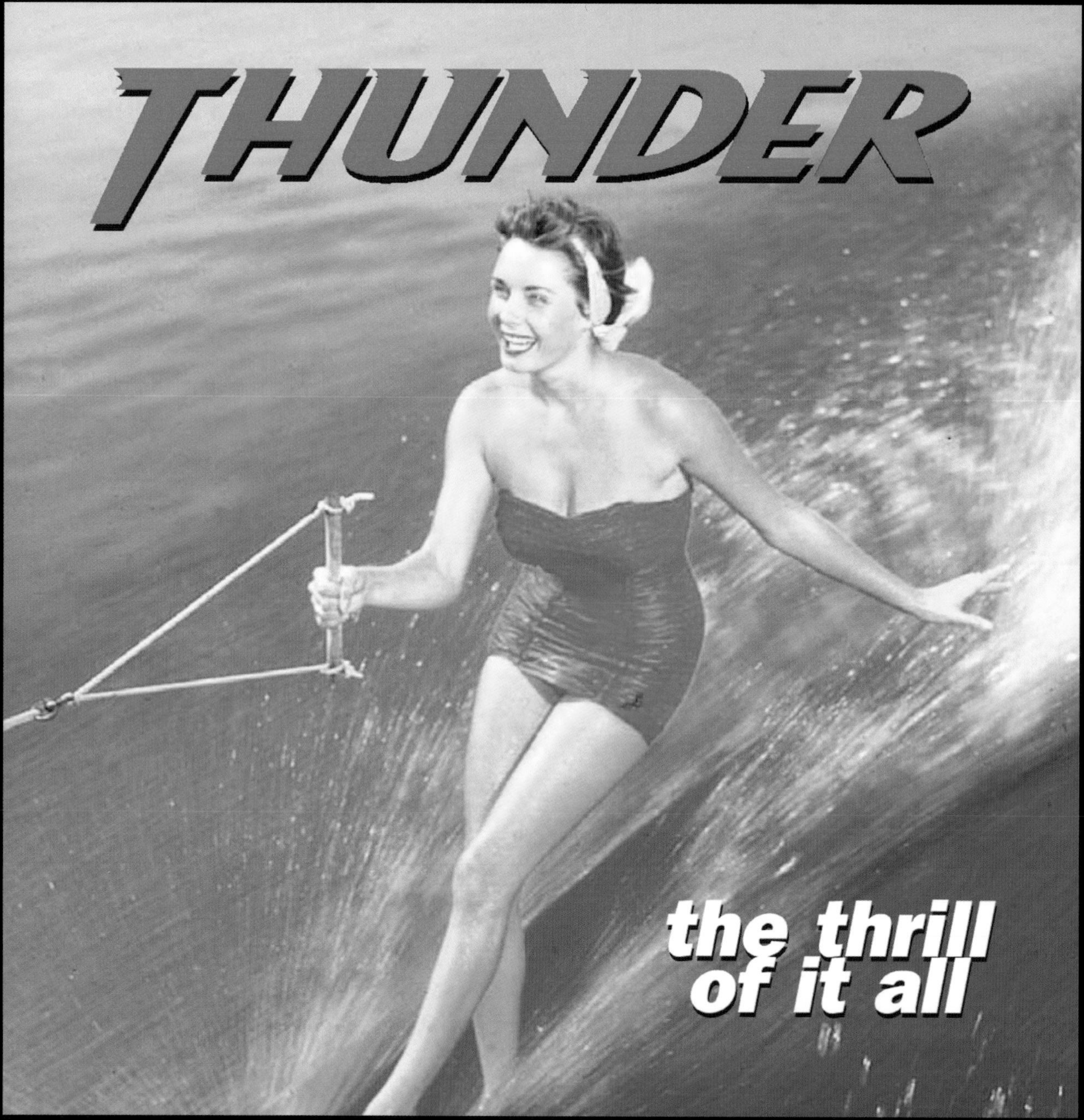
THUNDER
the thrill
of it all

THE THRILL OF IT ALL

SONG BY SONG BY LUKE MORLEY

Pilot Of My Dreams

I've written a lot of songs about watching women move. This is another one!

Living For Today

One of my favourite Thunder songs. I love the rolling 6/4 rhythm and the drama it creates. I got the inspiration for the first verse in Spain, looking at the sea from a high point on a nearby golf course.

Love Worth Dying For

It might be a cliché, but I like the notion that love can be more powerful than any self-preservation instinct. I think it's something we would all like to feel at some point in our lives.

Don't Wait Up

It's funny how people on the receiving end of irrational sexual jealousy sometimes end up doing the thing they're accused of. The guitar part owes more to James Brown than James Page, and the backing vocals add a hint of Motown.

Something About You

Harry came up with the 'Goodbye Johnny' idea, and it arrived just as Micke had decided to leave the band, so it was an easy lyric to write. I think we were all sad to see him go, but sometimes life makes decisions for you.

Welcome To The Party

If I'd known then what I know now, this would have been a very different lyric.

Tony Blair promised a lot, but delivered little and disappointed a whole generation. Hope is a dangerous thing! Harry came up with the top line and I fleshed it out from underneath.

The Thrill Of It All

This is about that point in a relationship where there's nowhere left to hide and you have to acknowledge the inevitable. Never pleasant, but necessary.

Hotter Than The Sun

I think this may have been inspired by the same woman as 'Pilot Of My Dreams'. It's a different groove for us, and another dabbling in the general area of funk. It may have had something to do with me working with The Power Station around this time. Certainly 'She's a sensual priestess, a lion in a dress' has more than a hint of Robert Palmer about it! Funny how some things are clearer years later...

This Forgotten Town

Harry came up with the chord sequence for the verse. The first couple of lines just popped into my head and that dictated the rest of the lyric. Ironically, this is much more of an accurate prediction of Blair's legacy than 'Party'.

Cosmetic Punk

This song is very uptempo for us, and a tip of the hat to Deep Purple with Benny's Hammond solo and the overblown tambourine à la 'Fireball'. I'm not really sure where the lyrical idea came from on this one. I don't usually care which side of the tracks somebody comes from, as long as they're honest about it. Maybe I'd met someone who was trying too hard to be 'street'. There's a lot of them working at record labels!

You Can't Live Your Life In A Day

The music business teaches you how to be patient and how to cope with disappointment, so being an optimist is definitely an advantage. You start out wanting to breathe the same rarefied air as your heroes, like the teenage boy in the second verse: "You've got your face against the window looking in". Unfortunately not everyone is cut out for it, and hope sometimes runs out for the more sensitive individual. Not the case with us, obviously!

Chris The recording of *Giving The Game Away* was pretty much a party with a recording session breaking out every now and then. I'll never forget the first shopping trip we did: Benny and I went to Tesco and came back with a trolley absolutely full of booze, plus a tube of toothpaste.

Danny We showed early on that we had a social conscience, with songs like 'Low Life In High Places', and we did a show in 1993 at the Brixton Academy with all profits going to Crisis. As a result, we've always received a lot of requests for us to take part in fundraising activities, play shows, donate auction items and so on. It's nice to help out where we can, but we'd never get any work done if we did everything, so, like a lot of bands, we're quite selective about the things we agree to do.

I got a letter in 1998 from a lady called Beverley Wears, who worked for the British Lung Foundation. She saw we were going to Newcastle on tour and suggested that we might wish to abseil from the top of the Tyne Bridge to raise money for her charity. Her letter was put together well, and I've always fancied a challenge – especially where there may be an element of danger – so I mentioned it to the band. Luke was having none of it and refused point blank, but the rest were all up for it, so I called her up and we made the arrangement. Thunder fans were very generous, and we raised a good chunk of money for the BLF.

Luke Normally I'm up for anything, but I'm not good with heights ever since I nearly stepped off some scaffolding when I was painting the outside of a house. I'm OK with widths: it's just heights I don't like!

Danny In actual fact, despite being quite high it was a pretty sedate descent, so while I enjoyed it immensely, I was a little bit disappointed by the lack of jeopardy. Beverley was there with her husband Paul, and they suggested that if I wanted a bit more of a thrill, perhaps I'd like to step it up and do a tandem free-fall jump out of a plane later that year. At this point both Harry and Chris ran away, but Ben's eyes lit up, and so it was arranged.

Once again Thunder fans gave generously, as did our friends, who said we

were mad, but we loved the idea of jumping out of a plane. The jump itself was the most exhilarating thing we'd ever done: scary as hell, but great. After we'd stopped begging the pilot to let us go up again, Ben drove home as fast as he could down the M11, with me hanging out of the sunroof shouting, "Faster, faster!" We've talked about doing it again, but so far it hasn't come to pass.

MCP Promotions by arrangement with Helter Skelter Presents
giving the game away tour '99
thunder
Plus Special Guests LUKAN

may 1999
tues 25th **leicester** arena
tel: 0116 255 5576
wed 26th **sheffield** city hall
tel: 01142 789789 / 665656
thurs 27th **leeds** town & country
tel: 0113 280 0100
sat 29th **norwich** uea
tel: 01603 764764 / 505491
sun 30th **manchester** apollo
tel: 0161 242 2560
mon 31st **glasgow** barrowland
C.C. tel: 0141 339 8383 (24 hours)

june
wed 2nd **newport** centre
tel: 01633 662866 (credit cards accepted)
thurs 3rd **london** shepherds bush empire
tel: 0171 771 2000
sat 5th **southampton** guildhall
tel: 01703 632601
sun 6th **cambridge** corn exchange
tel: 01223 357851
Tickets for all shows £11.50 except london £12.50,
available from venues and all usual agents
(subject to booking fee)

DEDICATED CREDIT CARD LINE TEL: 0115 912 9128 (24 hours, 100 operators)

For lowest booking fees - buy online and save at www.ticketweb.co.uk, Or by phone on 0171 771 2000.
For further information on Thunder contact their web site on: www.thunderchannel.com

Luke In 1998 we played with Status Quo, we did our own headlining tour through the UK and Japan, we released a cover of 'Play That Funky Music', abseiled off the Tyne Bridge, did a tandem free fall, skydived for the British Lung Foundation and did Christmas shows in London and Wolverhampton, which were filmed for the *Thunder Live* DVD released by Eagle. I'd say that's a fairly busy year. Who knew that a major change was around the corner?

Danny Around this time I went to the band and asked them straight if they would allow me to become the manager. That didn't happen at that point: nobody was very happy with the idea. They felt slightly uncomfortable with it. I think they thought there might be conflicts, and, I have to say, that got right up my nose. I explained that us having a manager was essentially like having a dog and

wagging the tail yourself, because I was making all the day-to-day and policy decisions.

Regardless of who was managing us, I was always the one who was in the middle. I knew how our business worked, and I was the one who signed the cheques, made sure the money was right and asked the questions of the tour manager, label and agent, so I knew a lot more about our business than the actual manager did. It became clear to me that there was no one else who had a vested interest in us the same way that I did, and who would put the work in to the degree that I would.

I got a lot of my business understanding from my old man, who had his carpet business and was a very persuasive salesman. He was very bright, perhaps frustrated by his lack of education, but he could sell anything to anyone, because he understood the psychology of selling. He made a lot of money out of his business, and he made a lot of mistakes, too. And in the end, he went bankrupt. It was interesting. He used to say to me, "You're like me, but you're harder. You're less concerned about the implications of your decisions." To this day, I don't know if that was a compliment or not.

As it happens, my attitude towards my father had begun to change. Back in 1992, I became a dad for the first time. It made me think about my own father a lot. He'd been very strict, and he used to hit me when I was a kid, but now I began to feel a little sorry for him. I realised that it must have been very hard for him to become a father at 19, and I asked myself how I would have dealt with it at that age. At the same time, he began to realise that he hadn't been the best dad, and he felt guilty about it, as he told me later on, but usually when steaming drunk. I always wondered why he had to get drunk to display any emotion other than anger.

Luke *Giving The Game Away* came out in March 1999 and we previewed it at the Wulfrun Hall in Wolverhampton. The second single, 'Just Another Suicide', was retitled 'You Wanna Know' for the UK market because Eagle thought that the radio wouldn't play a song with 'suicide' in the title.

Right: People occasionally accused us of arsing around. That's completely unjustified.

GIVING THE GAME AWAY

SONG BY SONG BY LUKE MORLEY

Just Another Suicide
I was in New York in 1997 rehearsing for The Power Station's US tour when I heard about the car crash in Paris that ended up being the end of Diana. Watching such a British event on American TV gave it all a slightly surreal feel, almost like watching a film. I started scribbling down a few ideas and a few weeks later Harry sent me over an idea that turned into the chorus. Obviously it's not actually about suicide.

All I Ever Wanted
A fairly bleak song about regret and admitting responsibility for moments of weakness that can ruin a perfectly good situation. It's unusual in that the chorus is fairly down for a Thunder tune and there are no big guitar sounds.

Giving The Game Away
I really enjoyed writing this one. A song is sometimes a good place to get things off your chest, and this is all about a particular record label person we had to deal with whose appetite for excess and glory was way worse than that of most musicians. It was a tip of the hat to The Beatles, musically, which is appropriate seeing as the person in question worked at EMI.

You'll Still Need A Friend
This is about realising things have run their course and wanting to be civilised about breaking up – whether it's a relationship or a band.

thunder you wanna know

Rolling The Dice
An important song as I managed to get a reference to golf into it! It's all about the ridiculousness of what we do for a living. Sometimes it's important to remind yourself how lucky you are.

Numb
One of my favourite Thunder songs, with a great vocal by Danny. I'm not really sure why it isn't more popular. Just goes to show what I know!

Play That Funky Music
I seem to remember we were playing in Holland at the end of a tour, and we spontaneously played this song during a soundcheck. It felt great, so we recorded it. It's fairly faithful to Wild Cherry's original. I remember Andy Taylor turning up while

we were recording this. We'd had a few drinks when we did the backing vocals, as you can probably tell. Harry was playing the fire extinguisher – I kid you not!

'Til It Shines
I think this is about materialism and superficiality, although I could be wrong... It's certainly a strange song.

Time To Get Tough
Another weird song: a bit schizophrenic – sort of Creedence meets 'Song 2' by Blur. It has a fairly tongue-in-cheek lyric about not putting up with other people's shit.

It's Another Day
All about reminding yourself that things could be worse, so enjoy yourself while you're here.

It Could Be Tonight
This was written with Taylor and Harry in Spain and it's all about the anticipation of the evening to come. Great things could happen! Taylor guests on acoustic guitar.

Harry We did the *Giving The Game Away* tour in May and June and then EMI released a B-sides album called *The Rare, The Raw And The Rest*. Meanwhile Luke did some gigs with Andy Taylor, but all was not well with Thunder, as they say.

Danny I felt by late 1999 that we couldn't compete, and I was very fed up. By then we'd been with Eagle for a couple of years, and before that it was Castle, and before that it was EMI. When you're with a major label and you go to an independent label, there's a marked difference, and when you put that against the backdrop of the time, which was very hard... we were ploughing a very lonely furrow at that point. So I decided in November 1999 that there was no point in going around in ever-decreasing circles, and I wasn't getting any younger. Basically, I'd had enough, and I told the band.

Chris That was a real shock, and a real disappointment. I really didn't want it to happen, because I'd only been in the band a couple of years. But right from the start I could see that Danny knew his onions, and I trust his decisions, so I didn't argue.

Luke Maybe we were starting to wind down a little towards the first split.

Ben I think we could have regained some ground, but I don't think it was a bad decision. I could see that we'd been on a downward spiral since the EMI days, and I've always thought that it's better to go out on a high.

Harry I remember *Kerrang!* being everything at one point, but we couldn't get them to write about us by 1999.

Danny When we broke up, it was my fault. It's always been my fault.

Luke I remember it being more of a joint decision. We sat down and talked about it and agreed that maybe we should stop for a while. It felt to me that no matter what music we came up with, or how well we

performed, there were no routes into mainstream media for us. We couldn't expand our audience, and I don't think we would have been happy just to hit a plateau after all those years. Other options might have seemed quite attractive, I suppose, although in my case I had no idea what I was going to do. I hadn't really thought about it.

Danny I was finding the singing very hard indeed. The thought of getting up every morning and doing it all over again was very difficult – I can't overstate that. To be honest, I had no great desire to sing at all any more. Mark Harris asked me if I

would production manage an MTV live show filmed for TV, and that looked interesting. I certainly had no intention of bringing Thunder back after a couple of years: in 1999 we were all young enough that we could do something completely new if we wanted to. My kids were aged from three to nine at the time and I could see our business shrinking. It seemed like the obvious thing to bring it to an end. We'd had a good run, so we couldn't really complain.

Harry We weren't as popular as we thought we should be, and we were running out of steam. The industry was in poor shape too.

Luke I was extremely frustrated with Eagle. I remember doing a showcase gig in Hamburg where there were supposed to be loads of journalists, but no one was there because the label staff hadn't got off their arses. They hadn't delivered their side of the bargain.

Danny There were no bands like us, so you couldn't get anybody to write about us, and if they did it was always slightly sneering and resentful. "Good old reliable Thunder..." – that was the way a lot of those pieces used to start. We knew they'd damn us with faint praise: it was quite hard.

The band were upset a lot of the time when we actually got reviewed. I used to say to them, "These people will still have jobs in years to come. You can't be horrible to them because they're only doing their job." At the end of the day, it doesn't matter as long as we maintain a good relationship with our fans. I don't really care about our popularity with the press: that will come and go. When they want to write about us, we should be gracious, and when they don't, we should be the same.

Luke I got a call from EMI in Japan asking if I wanted to make a solo album, and the honest truth is that I'd never considered it. I said yes before I'd really thought about it, which may have had something to do with the large cheque they were waving in front of me! I thought, "Fuck it, it'll be a challenge," and got into it. I decided to rent a place in southern Spain to complete the writing. I'd spent a lot of time there with Andy Taylor in 1995 and 1996 and I knew the area well.

Danny We did a farewell tour in December and one more gig on May 11, 2000, at Dingwalls in Camden. We did an acoustic set followed by an electric one, and filmed it all, but the video projector didn't work. All kinds of bullshit went on. The sound was dreadful and we all hated it. It wasn't a great way to end, although we did record the audio and the audience was great, as usual. We genuinely intended not to come back. We were done. For good!

Right: Backstage at the Forum in London, December 11, 1999.

2000–2004

WHAT THUNDER DID WITH THEIR TIME OFF, WITH SOLO ALBUMS AND — GASP! — REAL JOBS, BEFORE A TRIUMPHANT RETURN.

Danny It was a relief when Thunder was over. Everything stopped. We kept the band's bank account open, because we knew that income would still be coming in, and we were effectively still in business together, but we closed down our touring company. All the things that cost us money, we got rid of, keeping the bare minimum to keep us ticking over, and we got rid of the people who worked for us, one by one. In that period, I became the band's bookkeeper, to do the VAT returns.

Chris Harry and I played in a show called *Carnaby Street*, which was in the West End for about five minutes, and we played in some covers bands, and then I started working with Paul Young, which was great for a bass player. I was with Paul for a couple of years.

Ben I went back to my studio career again and struck up a good working relationship with Pete Brown, the Cream lyricist. Together we worked on some great records with some exceptional artists. Pete has a seriously good phone book and I got to work with people I really admired. This culminated in a John Lee Hooker tribute album sanctioned by the JLH estate after his death. It featured the likes of Peter Green, Jeff Beck, Jack Bruce and Gary Moore. While recording, Jeff Beck said to me, "You play a bit,

don't you?" I replied, "Not if you're in the room!" – he was exceptional. I recorded Tony McPhee too, but fortunately he didn't recognise me from the Toilet Tour days.

Danny I was working as a self-employed painter and decorator and doing other jobs: all the stuff I'd done before I was in the band. It was all word of mouth: my father-in-law was a great source of business because he was always down the golf club and had a massive network of friends. I also did the production management gig for MTV, working with Trevor Nelson, Brandon Block and the other big DJs. I did that for two years, around painting and working on building sites. I really enjoyed doing something very different. I still love getting the tools out and knocking something down now and then. It's good for the soul.

Then I got a gig as a production manager with Channelfly, who own the Barfly venues. Every time there was a gig at the Barfly, I would make sure that everything would be working OK and the shows got filed and recorded correctly. It was a real eye-opener. So many of the bands were shit. I found it quite funny.

It wasn't hard to switch out of rock star mode, because I'd never been in rock star mode. It doesn't really occur to me to be that way. I could give you loads of examples over the years of people coming up to me and

> **YOU CAN'T GET AWAY WITH AN INCH IN THIS BAND, AND YOU DEFINITELY CANNOT IN ANY WAY BELIEVE FOR ONE SECOND THAT YOU'RE A ROCK STAR.**

saying, "Are you Danny Bowes?" and I say no. I actually don't enjoy being recognised outside the band environment: it makes me very uncomfortable. Don't get me wrong – I love being in a band and singing onstage and seeing the crowd go nuts, but I never had any great desire to be famous. I just wanted to be successful, and make a few quid if possible. I think I'm very fortunate in that regard. My wife and kids always keep my feet on the ground – and also, in this band, if anyone starts getting above himself, we take the piss out of him something rotten.

I used to have my own dressing room when I was the only member of the band who didn't smoke, so I wouldn't breathe in all their pong, and the bastards used to come over, stick a big star on the door and write 'Elvis' underneath it. If I ever did any vocal warm-ups, they'd say, "Stop that. Who do you think you are?" You can't get away with an inch in this band, and you definitely cannot in any way believe for one second that you're a rock star.

I remember a huge row with Snake when he didn't have a spotlight on him at the Oxford Apollo, within six months of him joining the band. I wanted to sack him then, but Luke wouldn't let me, because he said we had a lot to do and the timing would have been awful. That's what we're like. We're so normal it's terrifying.

Luke We did a lot in 2000 and 2001, now I look back. I recorded a solo album, *El Gringo Retro*, with videos and singles; I played in Japan and the UK; and we released a video called *In Out Put The Kettle On* through the Thunder website. Then the final Dingwalls show came out as *They Think It's All Over... It Is Now* in July 2000.

Chris I played on Luke's solo albums, and the Bowes & Morley stuff, and on The Union too. I'm his go-to bass player, which is really nice: we've got a really good working relationship. He's a really good bass player himself, and he knows exactly what he wants.

Ben I helped Luke out with his solo album, playing keyboards and engineering. I had previously co-written a couple of songs with him and Andy in Spain, which made the album. I'm very proud of one of them: 'Paradise'. We went to Japan and toured it too.

Danny Before we were dropped by EMI in 1995, I was offered a solo deal by EMI's MD Jean-François Cécillon, who wooed me, saying, "I love your voice and I don't want to lose you." I said, "No problem, but I don't write. How are we going to get around that?" and he told me that I'd have the best writers, the best producers and so on. There was a lot of French hand-waving going on.

It was nice to be wanted, and he offered me some money, and so we did the deal. I did it on the strict understanding that I wouldn't leave Thunder, and that I wouldn't do it if that was his agenda. But after the deal was signed, EMI fired him, and I effectively became someone else's dirty washing. I spent the next three

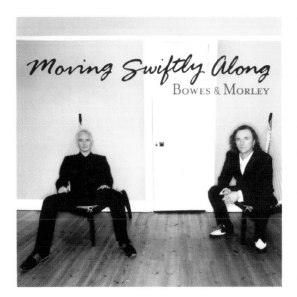
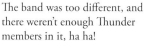

years going in and out of EMI, saying, "Can we make a record please?" and it all got a bit ridiculous, with them telling me to go and write some songs. I went down a lot of blind alleys with various writers and producers, and it just never happened.

About four years after that, I got a call from Shun Mori at EMI in Japan. He asked what was happening about the Danny Bowes solo album. I told him it was all but dead. He told me he would be very keen to help me make it, if I was still game. I thought about it for a few days, then called Luke and said to him, "Let's do an album and call it Bowes & Morley: you write the tunes and I'll sing them." He said, "Fine." It was my deal, but I needed him, so it made sense to make it a duo thing. We did two albums between 2000 and 2002. It was fine: a chance for us to stretch out a bit and do some shows between Thunder. The records were both good, although I don't think it ever really caught on with Thunder fans.

> **THE RECORDS WERE BOTH GOOD, ALTHOUGH I DON'T THINK IT EVER REALLY CAUGHT ON WITH THUNDER FANS. THE BAND WAS TOO DIFFERENT, AND THERE WEREN'T ENOUGH THUNDER MEMBERS IN IT.**

The band was too different, and there weren't enough Thunder members in it, ha ha!

Luke Danny was due to make a solo album for EMI, and I think he had a few problems in the writing area: he didn't enjoy doing it himself, and I had some songs written so I offered them to him, which is how Bowes & Morley evolved. The music was different to Thunder: it was more soul-oriented. I've always liked that kind of music, and it's fun to do things without the burden of expectation. That's what was nice about working solo and with Danny I could do whatever I wanted. I viewed these changes as opportunities rather than worrying about the future. I also enjoy producing and seeing how things come together in the studio, and obviously the new projects allowed me to do that. I didn't really say to myself, "Now what?" I just kept writing songs.

Harry I enjoyed making Luke's solo album, and touring it. It was lots of fun and quite removed from the Thunder experience, as well as being a nice change. I also played some gigs with a blues band called Bad Influence, and, after that, with Graham Bonnet and Don Airey. It was through Don that I made contact with Magnum, who asked me to join them in early 2002.

One early memory of Magnum was my first day in a rehearsal studio in Stourbridge. We went to the pub at one in the afternoon – and that's the last thing I remember about that day! We stayed there until that night, talking about mutual acquaintances and experiences. The following day, we actually played something, which sounded great.

MONSTERS OF ROCK

ALICE COOPER

THUNDER

THE QUIREBOYS

The DOGS D'AMOUR

Luke In July 2002 we announced that we were reforming for a tour called Monsters Of Rock in November, so our time away ended up only being a couple of years after all.

Danny I didn't want us to get back together! I was seriously busy with all my different jobs. What happened was this... Malcolm called me one day: he was working for Emap, the publishers, who owned the *Smash Hits* Live tour. He asked me to go up to Hull and sort out a merchandise problem which they were having up there on the tour. Apparently there was too much merch on display, and the guy looking after it had lost control of the situation. I said to Malcolm, "So you want me to be the merch policeman?" and he said yes.

Now, at these gigs I noticed the speed with which the pop acts switched over onstage and I thought, someone needs to do this for rock music, allowing for the fact that rock musicians actually need to play instruments. I thought about this all over Christmas 2001 and came up with a plan where the bands would share equipment to minimise changeover time. So I took it to Stuart Galbraith at Live Nation and explained why it would work, and he said, "OK. Find me a bill. We'll do it and I'll give you a percentage."

I went to our agent, Neil Warnock, and told him the plot, and he agreed to help me put a bill together with Stuart. Eventually we came up with Alice Cooper as headliner, The Quireboys to open and The Dogs D'Amour to go on second. Stuart said, "We need a special guest," and I said, "Who?" He said, "Thunder!" And I said, "No, no, no."

I didn't want to do it. I knew that we couldn't just do one gig, or even one tour, and that I'd end up involved in it all over again. I also knew that any love for the band from fans would dry up immediately if we came back and did a tour, then went away again. It would have been seen as a tour just for the money, and that's exactly what it would have been. So I resisted and resisted and resisted. I didn't even tell the band. In the end he said, "If you don't do it, I'm not doing the tour," and I thought, "Bollocks." I wanted to get the event off the ground, but I could see it disappearing before it even got going.

So I took it to the band for a decision.

Luke Danny suggested the Monsters Of Rock tour and we thought it would be a laugh, so we just went out and did it. We were only going to do those gigs, originally. The desire to make an album only came afterwards.

Danny Luke said, "Let's make an album!" and I thought, "Bollocks. I'm going to get caught up in all this again, and I won't be able to get out. I'll be like a hamster in a wheel." It really wasn't what I wanted to do. I actually wasn't sure if everybody would want to come back and do the gig: I was worried that they would be too busy.

By then I'd been working for Dave Stewart in a record label called Artist Network, looking after Jimmy Cliff – yes, the reggae giant. He was a lovely man, a real legend in every sense. The internet was emerging as a real force for communication, so I started to think that if we came back for the shows, maybe we could take our future into our own hands and release our own records.

Harry I missed playing with Thunder, of course, so when Danny suggested getting back together, and also managing the band, it was a no-brainer. We had a little cottage industry shaping up now, and we knew he was the man for the job. He's very good at what he does. We'd been fucked around by record companies so much in the past that it made sense to do it all ourselves.

Luke Most bands stop because there are insurmountable issues that prevent them from playing together, but that's never happened with us. We were friends who had stayed in touch, so it was easy to just say, "Let's give it another shot."

Danny So we ended up doing it. The shows with Alice Cooper were amazing. When we got back together to rehearse, it was like we were never away. It occurred to me afterwards as I was driving home. It didn't feel like a day had passed. It was very strange.

We also released a four-track EP, *Back For The Crack*, which we funded ourselves. We pressed up about 1,000 and sold out in three days, so we had to press more, and

then the idea of making an album seemed to make obvious sense. I hadn't wanted to reform and then go away again, because we would have been short-changing the fans and giving them false hope.

Mark I was the production manager for the Monsters Of Rock tour, for the three bands under Alice Cooper. Roger Searle had taught me a lot about tour managing: I'd go out on the road for a few days with the band and then head back to the office. Danny then asked me to become Thunder's tour manager, and I've been doing it on and off since then.

Luke We started recording a new album, *Shooting At The Sun*, in December 2002. In the end we decided to release it on our own label, STC Recordings.

Danny STC stands for Straight Talk Company, because I give you the news the same way: whether it's good or bad, I give it to you straight.

Chris Everything works with Thunder. Everybody has a role and everybody knows what they need to do. There are no egos in this band. I've worked with so many dysfunctional musicians who make everything hard work. Making music is a really joyful thing to do, and there's no need to make it difficult. That's how it is in Thunder. Danny is an extremely good manager, and one of the most switched-on people I've ever met. He's like a Bond villain, because he's very good at seeing opportunities and putting them together and he knows all the tricks. In fact I call him 'Daniel Blofeld', because I can imagine him sitting there stroking a white cat.

Luke Danny's got a very good brain. I think him becoming Thunder's manager was part of a natural progression for us. Being the singer in the band doesn't occupy him enough, and he doesn't contribute to the songwriting, which means he can focus elsewhere. He's a natural organiser and a natural negotiator, and he really enjoys that side of what he does.

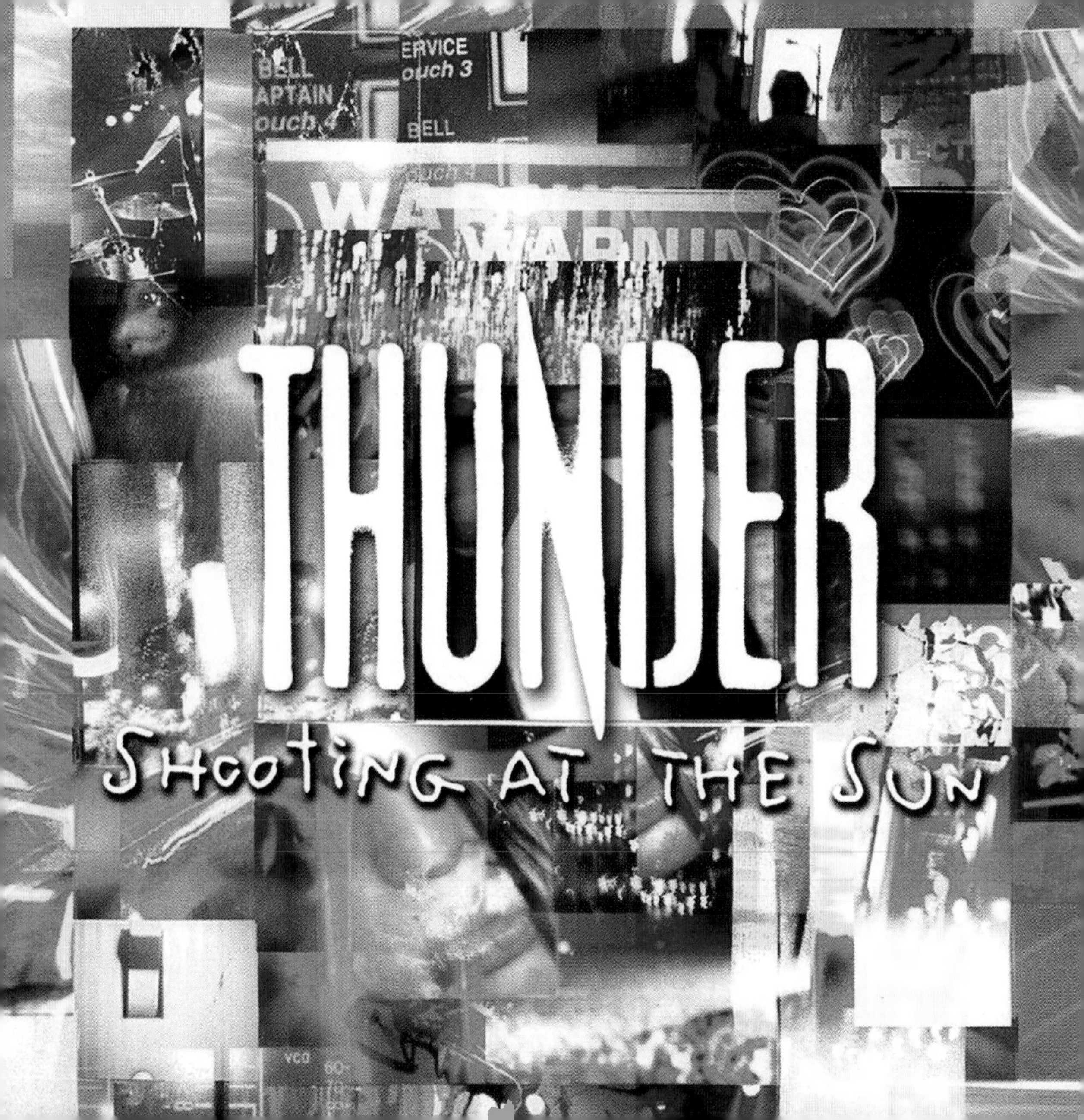
BELL
APTAIN
ouch 4
ERVICE
ouch 3
BELL
WARNIN
THUNDER
SHOOTING AT THE SUN

SHOOTING AT THE SUN

SONG BY SONG BY LUKE MORLEY

Loser

I was in a bar somewhere and I heard 'Somebody Else's Guy' by Jocelyn Brown, which has a very dramatic intro. I borrowed the concept and the whole song came from the intro idea. It's a song about low self-esteem, which may not be very rock'n'roll, but it's something that everybody understands. It was our first album after we got back together, and I wanted the opening track to be a statement.

Everybody's Laughing

I've spent a few evenings in the bar of the Sunset Marquis in LA, just people-watching. In Los Angeles lots of people purport to be advocates of a healthy lifestyle, but tend to visit the loo rather too much. Never having done cocaine, I was very naive about it until someone pointed out this curious behaviour to me. Thereafter, of course, I noticed it everywhere I went! Danny got the vocal in one take, I remember, which was impressive.

If I Can't Feel Love

About the difficulty some people have being demonstrative, and the problems it can cause.

Shooting At The Sun

All about futility. It's no fun being in love with someone who's in a relationship with someone else. Darkly funky.

The Pimp & The Whore

Talent contests, The X Factor? Don't get me started. This looks at the whole sorry business through the eyes of a Svengali-type character who is trying to manipulate his young charge into doing what he wants.

A Lover, Not A Friend

An angry post-relationship song. It's bad enough being dumped without discovering that the other person was completely dishonest all the time you were together.

Shake The Tree

A mate of mine spent a whole drunken evening telling me how sick he was of London and how he wanted to move out into the sticks. Eventually he did, but he was back in a couple of months! Be careful what you wish for.

Somebody Get Me A Spin Doctor

Wouldn't it be fun if we all had a personal spin doctor? Somebody to 'adjust the truth' on our behalf every time we fucked up or got caught with our trousers down. One of my favourite Thunder lines is in this song and goes: 'Napoleon wasn't short, he was only of diminished size'. We don't often play a shuffle-type groove, but we do here.

The Man Inside

This was written with Peter Shoulder, who came to the studio to help with the recording of this song and never left! He plays the cool Leslie guitar on this track. It was written about his ex-manager who was an interesting character, and is quite Beatle-esque.

Out Of My Head

Not the Kylie Minogue song! Not one of my better lyrics, to be fair...

Blown Away

This is about reaching a kind of crossroads in life, and the frustration and desperation of not knowing which direction to go in. It's in epic Thunder format, with gentle acoustic vibes exploding into a big riff.

Ben The 'Loser' single just missed out on the Top 40, which is pretty good for a band without a record label! We played with Deep Purple in Switzerland right after the release and then toured the UK, finishing up with two semi-acoustic Christmas dates.

Luke I love the Christmas shows. They are great, great fun, and it's nice to play other people's songs for a change.

Harry Those shows really took off. No other bands were doing that: we were doing cover versions, and doing them really well. Great fun!

Danny By 2004, we were now in a period where we were maintaining our own quality-control mechanisms. We wanted to be sure that everything was done to our own satisfaction, and we knew that we could do more or less anything we wanted, as opposed to previous years when we'd been subject to limits imposed by various record companies.

We spent a lot of money on a portable Pro Tools system so that we could plug everything in and record. I'd rented similar systems which weren't as good as ours, and I knew

THUNDER
Live at The Bedford Arms

how useful it would be to have the ability to record and mix our own records anywhere we wanted. This way all the Christmas albums could be done, and we did the *Robert Johnson's Tombstone* album in Spain. We did the *Bang!*

album in a castle. Costs were kept low and we didn't need to sell tons of records to make a profit. The downside is that you create a lot of work for yourselves, and the solution to that is to reach out to distributors, in the real world and online.

Luke Had we become a classic rock act by then? Well, it's weird. I think we fall between two generations, in a way. We're obviously not as old as Sabbath and Zeppelin and so on, but grunge and extreme metal came after us, so we sit in a weird place. I can't think of many bands like us who haven't split up. There was The Black Crowes, and the odd band like The Quireboys.

I get annoyed when people describe us as an Eighties band, because our first album didn't come out until 1990. I just think of us as an English rock'n'roll band. We get called 'rock legends' in the press sometimes, and I'm not sure about that, but it shows that people think of us in a certain way!

Below and right: Into the new millennium. Older and wiser, maybe; better, definitely!

2005–2009

BUILDING A CLOSE-KNIT ORGANISATION FROM THE GROUND UP – FOLLOWED BY IT'S GOOD NIGHT FROM US: PART 2.

Luke The old quote is true: songwriting is 10 per cent inspiration and 90 per cent perspiration. You have to work hard to write songs, but I take it seriously and I do knuckle down. If I'm writing, I work for six to eight hours a day. I sit there with a guitar and come up with a riff, a melody or some lyrics and off I go. Ideas have never been

hard for me: it's the discipline of getting the songs assembled.

That said, some albums come easier than others. The stuff I come up with in the first week is awful, usually, but once you're in the zone it comes out much more easily. You just have to get your brain in the process, and I found myself writing three studio albums in

the period between 2005 and 2009. The first of these was *The Magnificent Seventh*, which was released in the UK through our STC label, in Europe via Frontiers and by JVC in Japan, in February 2005.

Right: Rejected ideas for the sleeve of *The Magnificent Seventh.*

THE MAGNIFICENT SEVENTH

SONG BY SONG BY LUKE MORLEY

I Love You More Than Rock'n'Roll
This is a straight-up Thunder rock song that says a lot about our British roots, with elements of Free, The Rolling Stones and The Who. All of these align in four minutes of tongue-in-cheek simplicity that you can dance to.

The Gods Of Love
This song has an unusually dark riff for a Thunder tune. It features some equally unusual wah-wah bass from Chris, which started out as a daft experiment but which became the basis of the verses. The chorus states the obvious: when it comes to love, our lives are in the hands of fate, which can be cruel, sadistic and funny – but never predictable!

Monkey See, Monkey Do
The music industry has changed immeasurably since we began making albums. There used to be people working at major labels who cared about music and understood that talent is not something you can manufacture. In the mid-Nineties, the majors began to employ people from a corporate background who knew how to mass-market Coca-Cola but plainly didn't understand what makes music great. The upshot of all of this was a lot of manufactured pop, which was good for the chart profile and the annual shareholders' meetings, but which produced very little music of lasting quality. Then along came the internet, which allowed and encouraged creativity and individuality, and made the majors very worried – so worried that they frantically began to downsize and restructure. This song gets inside the head of an upwardly mobile record executive as his position becomes increasingly futile. We attempted to make it sound like an out-of-control juggernaut to echo the dinosaur sentiment.

I'm Dreaming Again
Here's an unashamedly sentimental song about looking back regretfully at a relationship that went wrong. I think this is what people call a power ballad!

Amy's On The Run
I'm not quite sure how I ended up with a lyric about a pre-op transsexual, but that's what happened. I can't imagine the desperation that people in this situation feel, but I tried to see it with a sense of humour. There's definitely a hint of Boston on the outro but that's because we recorded it near there. Boston, Lincolnshire, that is.

The Pride
A good old-fashioned half-time bruiser built around a 'heavy' riff in the true sense of the word, although the first section of the solo does get quite jazzy for a second or two. I do mean only a second or two...

Fade Into The Sun
Big power chords and dynamics are a backdrop to a lyric about how the wrong kind of relationship can crush your self-esteem and confidence to the point where you feel transparent. Someone in the band said the intro reminded them of 'Delilah'. Well, I suppose it is quite melodramatic.

Together Or Apart
A 'typical epic Thunder ballad' is how you would describe this. The quiet and the loud, the whisper and the scream, the caress and the grope, and so on. Lyrically, it's about an ultimatum that many people will have heard from a partner.

You Can't Keep A Good Man Down
A song to raise the spirits in a heads-down, no-nonsense kind of way. Good for breaking the speed limit to. It's a very simple piece of rock'n'roll: I can't remember the last time we were this uncomplicated.

One Foot In The Grave
An uptempo, bluesy tune all the way from the swamp-infested delta that is south-east London. It's all about somebody who can't stop worrying and complaining obsessively about every minute detail of their life, so much so that their life hardly seems worth living to the observer.

One Fatal Kiss
This was co-written one very pleasant afternoon with Russ Ballard. I'm sure he has a portrait of Dorian Gray in his attic. It's easy to hear his input on this song and it was nice to have someone of his ability involved. The result is a very mid-tempo – dare I say it, AOR – tune with a good shout-along chorus.

Danny We started getting creative with the STC label, reissuing albums such as *They Think It's All Over* and *They Think It's All Acoustic*, as well as releasing the *Six Shooter* EP through the internet. 'I'm A Lucky Man' was our first download single in June 2005. We also played some great shows that year, touring Europe, headlining the Rock & Blues Custom Show in Derbyshire and doing an acoustic set at the Hawk Kawasaki party at Brands Hatch. We put out our first couple of concert DVDs too, and Luke wasted no time in writing an eighth album. We were flying at this stage, having come to understand how the business of running a label and a management company works.

Luke It carried on into 2006. We did a UK tour in January before heading back to Japan and then Europe, before doing festivals here and abroad with Deep Purple, Alice Cooper, Journey, Ted Nugent, Status Quo and Dr Feelgood.

The next album, *Robert Johnson's Tombstone*, was a bit different. As a songwriter, you can't be afraid of making a cock of yourself: you have to try new things to stay motivated and keep it exciting, and sometimes those things don't work. The more you do it, the better you become, like any craft. The problem with many bands of a certain age is that they lose interest in making albums: they become simply an excuse to tour. It's never been that way for me; I've enjoyed making the albums equally.

Robert Johnson's Tombstone came about when I was helping Andy Taylor's son, who is a talented musician, with some demos and advice, down in Exeter. I was driving home and listening to one of those late-night Radio 2 programmes about the blues. The guy was talking about the blues musician Robert Johnson and the stories about a bottle of poison, a bottle of whisky and a prostitute being involved in his death, and I thought, "This is so rock'n'roll!" So I got home and started researching Johnson, and it went from there.

Left: Ben, Luke and neighbour Scottish Bill in May 2006 at the villa in Mijas, Spain, where much of *Robert Johnson's Tombstone* was recorded.
Above: Photo session with Jason Joyce.
Below: Rejected ideas for the *Robert Johnson's Tombstone* sleeve.

THUNDER

ROBERT
JOHNSON'S
TOMBSTONE

ROBERT JOHNSON'S TOMBSTONE

SONG BY SONG BY LUKE MORLEY

Robert Johnson's Tombstone

This song doesn't have a verse, a bridge or even a chorus but it's one of the most exciting things we've done. It's all about the mythology surrounding the legendary and influential bluesman. I knew a bit about him as a big influence on Eric Clapton, but it wasn't until I was listening to a programme about the blues on Radio 2 that I heard about the legend and the myth. Nobody actually knows exactly how and why he died so young, or where he's buried, but everybody agrees it had something to do with drinking and womanising. His ability as a guitar player caused many of his contemporaries to claim he'd sold his soul to the devil in exchange for his extraordinary guitar technique. Either way, all the ingredients in his story, true or false, make it a great one to tell and embellish.

Dirty Dream

We've all had an improper dream about a person we know, but who we had never really considered in 'that' way. Normally you would deal with it by not mentioning it to anyone, pretending it never happened and getting on with your life. The poor fool in this song, however, becomes obsessed with the object of his forbidden desire.

A Million Faces

An epic Thunder ballad. This song is written from the point of view of somebody trying to comfort a friend whose relationship has gone terminally wrong. There's plenty more fish in the sea, after all!

Don't Wanna Talk About Love

This could be about the victim of the previous song. It's about someone who is so traumatised by their last relationship that they can't and won't talk about it.

The Devil Made Me Do It

The first song written for the album. It's all about temptation. The subject here has no problem succumbing to everything, and then simply blames every single act or deed on the influence of the devil. I wish I could have got out of some of my past misdemeanours that easily!

Last Man Standing

This was Chris's first Thunder co-write. He came up with a terrific riff and title that inspired the whole thing. Regardless of what you think about Bush, Blair, Saddam Hussein and the war in Iraq, there is one absolute truth amid the spin and deceit that we have been fed, which is that lots of innocent people have died, and that more will die. As the man or woman in the street, we can only process the information available to us and, as turned out to be the case with Weapons of Mass Destruction, that information is often tainted. You can't justify going to war on poor intelligence and hearsay. I'm not usually an advocate of politics in rock'n'roll, but when it's on the news every day, we can't just look the other way and pretend it's not happening. I hope the tune is as epic as the subject it addresses.

Chris Strange but true: I wrote that riff after watching a film called *Fahrenheit 9/11*, which addresses the topics that Luke eventually wrote about. But Luke had no idea that I'd seen it, or what had inspired the riff – there were no lyrics, and the title came from another song which I'd sent him. Odd.

My Darkest Hour

This song is unlike anything we've ever done before. It's very simple musically in that it consists of only one acoustic guitar, cello and voice. It's a melancholy song about regret and not being able to change mistakes made in the past. Quick, pass the Kleenex.

Andy Warhol Said

You would have to have been living under the sea or on another planet not to have noticed the explosion in 'celebrity' media over recent years. I know we've always had a fascination with the lifestyles of the rich and famous, but it's now got so out of control that the press are having to invent new 'celebs' on a daily basis to satisfy a demand that they themselves created. This means that literally anybody can claim the dubious mantle of celebrity. This song ponders the possibility that Andy Warhol's prediction that 'everybody will be famous for 15 minutes' has come true.

What A Beautiful Day

Being the old romantic that I am, I've always wondered about the possibility of falling in love at first sight. It's never happened to me, but I like to think it does for some people. The guy in this song is so overwhelmed by a woman he sees in the street that despite the diabolically bad weather, he perceives it to be a 'beautiful day'.

It's All About You

It's not a nice place to be when you're with somebody whose interest is visibly waning, especially when they deny it. It's the height of selfishness to prolong something when you've lost interest, even though a part of you thinks you're sparing the other person's feelings. If it's over, admit it and move on, damn it!

Stubborn Kinda Love

I'm sure a lot of people will have experienced a love/hate-type relationship at some point. This kind of relationship can be very tiring and a lot of hard work, but at the same time very passionate and exciting. I suspect it's the latter that makes it last, although a sudden implosion is always a possibility.

Danny By now we were a fully fledged organisation, although we do things a bit differently. Luke and I are very different people. I'll have a row with anyone anytime, and once it's done it's forgotten because I don't bear grudges. I think Luke would rather run a hundred miles than argue with anyone: he's the Henry Kissinger of rock! But because of that, he can rely on me to have a row, and I can rely on him to be diplomatic.

As the son of a retailer, it was natural for me to be interested in the business side of music, so when we went to see the manager or the accountant or the tour manager, I would always want to sit with them and say, "So how does that work?" I never had any real interest in writing music, whereas Luke's obsessed with it.

We decided that rather than do another album straight away, we would do three six-track EPs instead. They sold well, and we

made a box for the third one that the previous two would go in. It worked well.

Our friend Margarita told us we could use her castle to record if we wanted to, so after the EPs, we shot back down the M4 with the gear. The result was the *Bang!* album.

Ben Recording at the castle was a real experience. Taking our Pro Tools rig and a big box of microphones, we turned one castle turret into a control room and another turret into a recording studio. Linking them with a long cable, I had to climb up and run it along the top of the castle walls. It felt like we were following in Deep Purple's footsteps – 'Smoke In The Castle'? I was told that recording in a circular turret was a no-no, but I disagree – the drum sound was amazing, much akin to John Bonham's sound on *Physical Graffiti*. The only problem was that the studio, being a castle, was freezing cold. Poor old Luke and Harry had to bear the worst of it as the control room had all the heaters, and that's where I was.

Above: A rejected idea for the *Bang!* sleeve.
Below and right: Promo shoot at Walton Castle where *Bang!* was recorded.

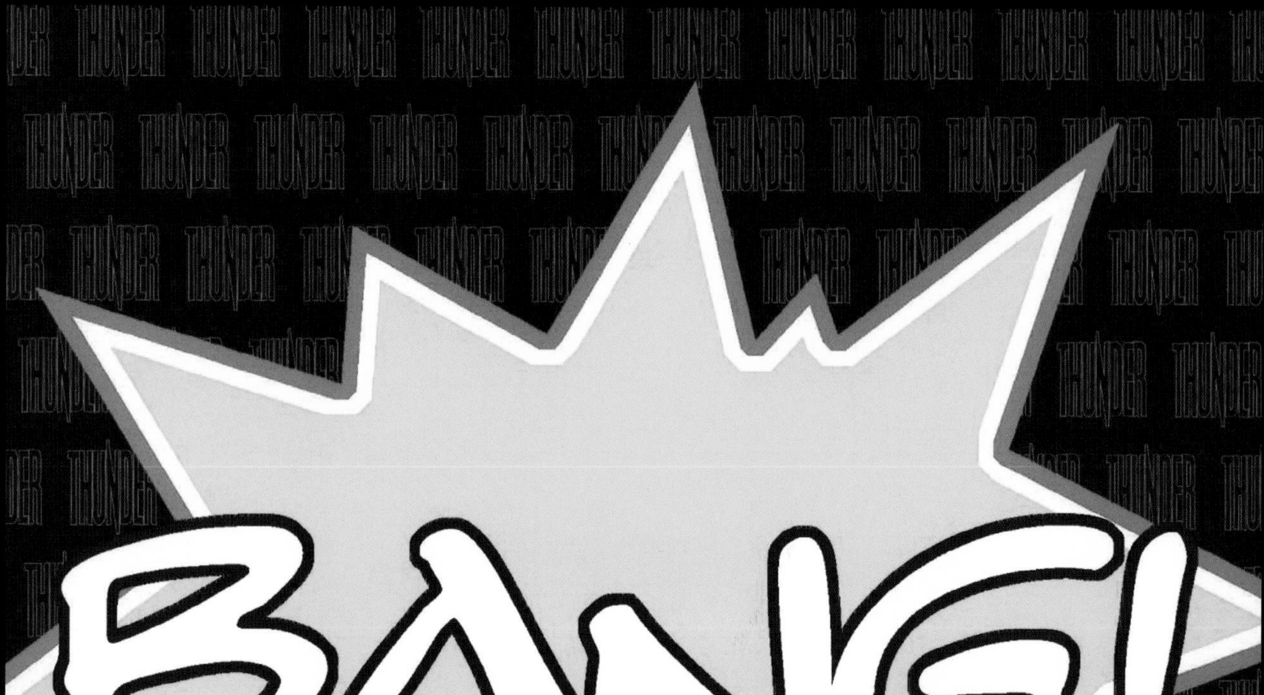
BANG!
THUNDER

SONG BY SONG BY LUKE MORLEY

On The Radio
I'm not one to moan or complain. We're very lucky to have had the career we've had to date, but there's one thing that really aggravates me: we've never, ever had enough, if any, support from mainstream English radio. Over the last 20 years we've watched other bands have their moment in the sun as far as daytime radio play goes, but we've never been afforded that luxury. I think it's the main reason the band isn't better known. Maybe it's just because we're about as far from cool, hip and trendy as it's possible to be! Anyway, rather than get down about it, I thought I'd write a song about it and keep my sense of humour (and my sanity) intact.

Stormwater
Anyone who saw what Hurricane Katrina did to New Orleans couldn't help but be moved by the plight of its residents. I was lucky enough to spend three days there in 1997, and it's a very special city with a unique vibe due to the mixture of cultures that form its history. It's also alive with music and it affected me greatly.

Carol Ann
Now don't get me wrong, I like a drink. However, the consequences of excessive drinking have to be dealt with when one is probably least prepared to do so – the morning after, when you have an awful hangover. I'm not proud to admit it, but there have been times when I don't remember anything that happened beyond a certain point in the previous evening. This tells the story of a guy who wakes up remembering nothing and the only clue he has is a name and a phone number scrawled on the back of his hand in lipstick! Let he who is innocent cast the first stone...

Retribution
You know how it is when nothing's going your way: it can feel as if fate's got it in for you. This song is quite jazzy and oscillates between 5/4 and 6/4, two very unusual time signatures for us – and torture for Harry. Maybe that's why I like it so much. Nice!

Candy Man
In my spam email folder I once found an invitation to meet Olga and Svetlana, two very beautiful Russian girls looking for English husbands. Obviously I leapt onto a plane for Moscow immediately. No, I didn't really – but the guy in the song does.

Have Mercy
An uncomfortable subject for any man over a certain age, myself included! It's a racing certainty that one day you will find yourself gazing at a beautiful young woman. There's nothing wrong with that, but when somebody informs you that the object of your lustful daydreaming is still of school age, it's a whole different thing. This awful moral dilemma is the inspiration behind many great blues songs, and I had to get to 47 to truly understand what they were going on about!

Watching Over You
This was written with Andy Taylor and Mike Keen. Not *that* Andy Taylor, but his son Andrew Junior. Strange, since I've known Andrew since he was no more than an ankle-biter! Seriously, though, he is a chip off the old block and has his father's instinct when it comes to melody and crafting a good song. This song appeals to me because the lyric can be interpreted as a mournful ballad or as something a little darker, bordering on obsession. You decide: a romantic, shy fool or a pervy stalker.

Miracle Man
I have no problem with religion. Whatever floats your boat is fine with me, providing it doesn't impact on my life. This song is about the kind of people who use religion to relieve you of your money by means of fear and/or false promises of redemption, in exchange for a lump of cash. Anyone who has cable television or has visited the southern USA will have seen evangelists whipping up a storm on the 'God' channels. Some of them are performers of considerable talent. It's just a shame that they decide to use their skills this way.

Turn Left At California
I've always been a fan of the road movie genre: wide-open spaces, endless highways... you know the sort of thing. I'm also particularly fond of sitting in the shade somewhere hot with an ice-cold beer. This song combines the two in a strange, hypnotic Tex-Mex-flavoured, meandering epic. It's unlike anything we've done before.

Love Sucks
You have to retain your sense of humour at all times when dealing with the opposite sex, because there are no absolutes and no certainties, and the thing you least expect will probably be what happens next. Why do we do it to ourselves? Human relationships defy analysis, but if they didn't exist what would I write about?

One Bullet
In recent years there have been God knows how many young people murdered by shooting or stabbing in London. I live in London, I grew up here, and it disturbs me greatly that this is happening. Being young should be a time in your life when you're free not to worry. We all need to do something about it in whatever small way we can.

Honey
A pet hate of mine are magazines like *Hello!* and *OK!* I don't think they have a positive effect on those who read them, because they glorify the mundane and the vacuous. This song is about a guy who's so fed up with his girlfriend's material obsessions that he can't take any more. He terminates the relationship and spews out all the bile that he's kept in check for so long. It's a major catharsis.

Danny Our operation got bigger as our catalogue grew, and after six or seven years of this, it took me to the edge of a nervous breakdown. I was doing all the deals, managing all the online stuff, and I pretty much had a broom hanging out of my arse so I could sweep the floor at the same time. It wasn't that the jobs were difficult, I just didn't have enough hours in the day to do them all, and it's very hard to find assistance that is worth the money. At one point I actively sought management for the band: we had a couple of conversations that didn't really go anywhere.

For the record, both times we split up, it was not with the intention of coming back. The first time we all agreed it was the right thing to do, and the second time I felt I had to stop. I was done in after six-plus years of managing the band and running the label. Neil Warnock, our agent at the time, offered me a job as an agent in his company. I tried it for a few months in a part-time capacity, but it should have been obvious to me from the get-go that it wouldn't work doing both jobs. It just shows how strung out I was. I got to the point at Christmas 2008 where I couldn't go on, and something had to give. I had kids coming up to university age, and I had to make my life simpler. I decided I had to leave the band. I didn't want to, but I felt I had to.

Harry That was a very disappointing meeting. Danny was burned out and he needed a change of direction. I didn't see it coming at all. We all sat down around the table at Chris's house in Chelmsford and said, "Right, this is what we want to

> **WE BOWED OUT WITH SOME GREAT GIGS. YOU CAN PUT THE HAMMERSMITH SHOW DOWN AS ONE OF MY ALL-TIME MOST MEMORABLE SHOWS. WE WERE GREAT!**

achieve this year," and Danny said, "I'm sorry to say this, but I'm going to call it a day. I've been offered this job and my kids are at university. I need a new challenge and a regular income, so I'm going to go for it." He was asking for our blessing, and we respected that, but we weren't very happy about it – although I have kids and I understand the need for an income. These are my mates: they know everything about me and we've been through a lot of ups and downs together. I remember feeling devastated once it had all sunk in.

Danny There was much more of a debate about calling it a day this time. I remember the conversation. Luke was adamant that he didn't want to continue. Harry and Chris wanted to continue. Ben was ambivalent, initially, but in the end he sided with Luke. I knew they were fed up, but they were very reasonable, and they understood my reasons.

Chris I never want to stop playing with Thunder because it's so much fun, so I was completely gutted. Again.

Danny I suggested to them in all seriousness that they could get another singer, and I would get them gigs. I meant it, and I wouldn't have blamed them, though deep down I think I secretly hoped they wouldn't replace me.

Luke We had the discussion about whether we should try and find another singer, and we decided that we wouldn't. I didn't think that was a good idea. Danny's voice is an integral part of the band's sound, and it would just be wrong. I also

thought, perhaps selfishly, that it would be a chance to do something else, and I'd been working with Peter Shoulder for some time on various things, which is how my band The Union came about.

Ben The meeting took place at Chris's house. I noticed that Danny wasn't his usual self as we started discussing our regular business, and after we'd finished, he dropped the bombshell. He left us to discuss the situation further, which we did.

Harry We discussed getting another singer, but it wouldn't have worked. We decided to wait and see what happened and see if Danny missed the band – and after a couple of years, he did.

Ben I knew there was no one who could take Danny's place. For me, it wasn't an option. I believed that everybody in the band was irreplaceable by this point anyway. I was lucky in that I had a fallback career as an engineer.

Danny We announced the split, and a series of shows to see us on our way, and say our goodbyes to fans. It was very emotional for both them and us. We put a brave face on it and stayed professional, and the shows were very emotionally charged. It was hard to do it, and I was relieved when it was over, but also very sad.

Harry We bowed out with some great gigs. You can put the Hammersmith show down as one of my all-time most memorable shows. We were great!

Left: Taking a break during a soundcheck.
Overleaf: A few shots from Hammersmith 2009: the *20 Years And Out* tour comes to a spirited and emotional climax!

2010–2016 AND BEYOND...

BACK AND STRONGER THAN EVER, THUNDER DEFEAT THE EVIL MUSIC INDUSTRY ON THEIR OWN TERMS. CAN ANYTHING STOP THEM NOW?

Harry When we split in 2009, because Danny wanted a change of career, we didn't know if Thunder would ever resurface. He didn't want to let any of us down, and he wanted to be sure that we were all going to go on to do other things, but, at the same time, he had to do what he had to do. I went out and joined Snakecharmer, and also I was asked to play in Jim Cregan's band.

Ben Once again, I turned to my recording studio career: I really didn't fancy playing in any other bands because Thunder had been so special and easy to be in. I didn't trust anyone else to offer me that kind of life. I did try my hand at live mixing for a Pink Floyd tribute act, but realised it wasn't for me.

Chris Again, I had no desire for the band to stop: it was still the most enjoyable gig I'd ever been in. I managed to keep busy – in between touring with Russ Ballard, Don Airey, Colin Blunstone and The Union, Harry and I were involved in a project called Shadowman, with Steve Overland from FM and Steve Morris. We've recorded five albums without ever doing a show – it must be some kind of record!

Previous page: Harry about to perform the ritual throwing of the drumstick into the audience at Hammersmith Odeon in 2009. It will always be the Odeon to us**.**
Above: The Union's second album, *Siren's Song.*
Right: Luke with his partner in The Union, Peter Shoulder.
Overleaf: Just when you thought it was all over... Back from retirement (again) for a one-off at High Voltage festival, London in July 2011. Hot day, great crowd and sunburn all round!

Luke A couple of days after Danny told us what he wanted to do, I went to see a band in Camden and Pete Shoulder was there. I'd known him since 2001, when I'd been looking for a bit of co-writing and his music was recommended to me. We got chatting and I told him that Thunder were going to part ways. We decided to form a band, The Union, and make an album – as simple as that. It came out in August 2010.

Malcolm I managed The Union for their first album. Luke had mentioned that he was putting together a new band, so I emailed him with some ideas to consider. The management company where I worked at the time had considered financing the album, so I told him

> **WHEN WE SPLIT IN 2009, BECAUSE DANNY WANTED A CHANGE OF CAREER, WE DIDN'T KNOW IF THUNDER WOULD EVER RESURFACE.**

that authentic classic rock and blues was very easy to market, and he had been thinking the same thing, so it evolved. I think Luke thought that my input would be valuable, but Pete didn't: he thought I was just a money man.

Luke Chris played bass and a guy called Phil Martini from Down'N'Outz played drums. It was good for me because Pete brings different influences to the band, like Tom Waits and Neil Young, to the ones I have. We wrote a lot of songs in a short period of time: stuff was getting written and it seemed like the right thing to do to get it released. We did two albums and a live DVD – we played Sonisphere, High Voltage and Download and we toured with Whitesnake and Thin Lizzy, all in the space of two years.

Considering that it was entirely self-financed, the band did well: the albums still tick over now. When Thunder became a possibility again, I told Pete that I needed to go off and do it to keep the coffers filled, and that it would be a perfect time for him to go off and do a solo album. It would be nice to play with him again, but Thunder is out of control again now and finding the time might be difficult!

Thunder came back in 2011, at least briefly. As is always the case, someone asks us to play a show, and if it sounds good and the money is right, we come back together and do it. In this case it was the High Voltage Festival in July 2011.

Harry High Voltage was great, although it was too hot onstage! Money-wise we did very well, and it was great to get back together again.

Luke We get asked to do a lot of festivals, and I think it's because we're the kind of band who can play a set that will send a large crowd home feeling good. We've always been comfortable playing for large crowds. All those years playing pubs gave us the stagecraft we needed, going all the way back to when I saw Bruce Springsteen with Danny with CBS back in the mid-Eighties. He did it so consummately that you felt like he was sitting in a pub playing to you. His grasp of dynamics – all the pushes and pulls in the set that go from quiet to loud, and how many times to go round on a chorus, and so on – was just so amazing. At one point he came out with an acoustic guitar and sang by himself, and controlled the audience by himself. He knew exactly how to help an audience enjoy itself, that's the best way I can describe it, and that's what we try to do, too.

Danny The strange thing was that, although we weren't making records or touring, we still spoke all the time, and I continued to look after our business, so although it was much simpler with nothing going on, it didn't actually feel that different. We didn't fall out, and we were offered shows every five minutes, but we turned them all down. The other guys were busy doing other things, and having decided an agent's life was not for me in 2010, I started managing other bands.

The High Voltage show was the one we gave in on, and it was amazing. There were so many Thunder fans wearing our shirts in the crowd, and all of them singing every word of every song. That led to the 2011 Christmas show at Rock City in Nottingham, which became two because the first one sold out so quickly. It felt like we were back, albeit just for two shows, and I started to realise just how much I'd missed it.

Luke After The Union had parted company with Malcolm, I found myself doing a lot of the things that Danny does for Thunder, and I really didn't want to do them! But somebody had to. I can take care of the business side, but I don't particularly enjoy it. I found myself looking at too many spreadsheets, which Danny does very well indeed. He's the kind of person who likes to understand why things work and the order that things come in, and that's very important for a manager.

Danny I was contacted in 2011 by a volunteer at a secondary school in Maidstone, asking if I would go down and talk to the kids there about the music industry. I said yes, and asked the band if any of them would come along and keep me company. They all said no, but Ben took pity on me and said he'd do it.

We went down there and sat in front of the kids, telling anecdotes and making them laugh, and then had to do it all over again at the end because a whole other load of kids came pouring in. The guy had stitched us up! Afterwards, we were driving home and agreed we'd both enjoyed the experience.

A few weeks later I was having lunch with my friend Steve from Live Nation, who was nagging me about doing some live shows. After a bit of thought, and remembering the school experience, I suggested that I do a spoken-word two-man show with Ben, plus some tunes for the audiences to sing along with – like stand-up comedy but with songs. I persuaded Ben to come and see Steve for a meeting, but on

the day of the meeting Ben texted me to say that he had a hangover and couldn't come because he was throwing up everywhere. I said, "There's money involved and it's all arranged, so put the coffee on and I'll be over to pick you up in an hour."

When I got there, he looked like the oldest man in the world: he couldn't even speak. When we got to Live Nation I told him that he had to shine like a Christmas tree as soon as we went in, and that he could die later. To his credit he did it: he lit up and we made Steve laugh. At the end I said, "Well?" and Steve said, "I'll do it!" And off we went, around the country in January 2012. We billed ourselves as 'Danny & Ben From Thunder' and did 15 shows that month.

People seemed to like it, and we were crying our eyes out with laughter that people would pay us to do it, because we didn't actually think it was much good! It was a little bit nerve-wracking but we had a lot of laughs. Essentially we just exercised our wit as we would do on the tour bus, but in front of a crowd. The music changed, too, because I sang it in a different key and we did different arrangements to the Thunder style. We went back and did a load more dates the following January, and got away with those too. It was so different to anything else we'd done, and such good fun – we loved it.

Ben Outside of Thunder, the Danny & Ben show was without a doubt the most fun I've ever had. I've always enjoyed making people laugh, and here I was doing it onstage. Being expected to speak during a show was a little strange at first, but I got it in the end. When Danny first approached me about it, I thought he was completely mad and that nobody would turn up, but once again I was proved wrong. Recording the songs was a very interesting exercise. Rearranging Thunder songs for one instrument, changing keys and arrangements was a real challenge. I think it taught Danny a lot about his voice, as he was using it in a very different way.

Harry I've generally escaped any drumming-related health problems, but I did have the mitral valve repaired in my heart in 2012. I felt ill for a couple of weeks and then checked myself into hospital. They said, "We need to repair your mitral valve," and I said, "Oh no!" They said, "It's all right, we do two or three of these a day," and I said, "Oh, OK then." They told me I needed to take a few months off drumming, but, as you'd expect, I was back on the drum stool a few weeks later.

Above and right: It's beginning to look a lot like Christmas. The 2012 Christmas shows in fact.

Danny We were very concerned for Harry, but he took it all in his stride and appeared to go through the op and the recovery period afterwards as if it was the most normal thing in the world. Stoic of south London. Once he was back to his athletic best, we did the 2012 Christmas shows at Manchester Academy. Luke and I had dinner just before, and agreed it might be good if we asked our agent to look for maybe six festivals for 2013. I didn't want the others to just drop what they were doing, but if there was a way to do just a few shows without mucking things up for them, perhaps it could work.

Once the word spread, the show offers came flooding in. We were concerned what fans might think about us, coming back for shows only, and some naturally thought we'd done the whole thing on purpose, as if it was planned, splitting up purely to reunite later on. Luckily, most people understood that we're as prone to the pressures of daily life as everyone else. At that point it was still not in our minds to make another album: that happened at the end of the shows in 2013.

Luke We were asked to play opening slots with Whitesnake and Journey in 2013, and we played Download too. Those shows were unbelievable! We were only doing 45-minute sets and we knew we'd be in the bar by 8 p.m. We had underestimated the value of Thunder to the punters: everywhere was full up when we went on. It was overwhelming sometimes: we literally couldn't play for a couple of minutes at the start of the Cardiff show because of the volume of the crowd. We hadn't anticipated that reaction at all, so I said to Danny, "We should make a record, because we may not get this kind of opportunity again."

Harry People were saying to me, "What's happening with Thunder?" and I said that we were still in semi-retirement, just doing gigs now and again. I was busy with Magnum, Luke had The Union, Danny was managing, Benny was a studio engineer and Chris was out doing gigs. If I'm truthful, at the Whitesnake and Journey shows, we appeared to go down better than the headlining bands. I think it's safe to say that we blew them away. That got the old brain box ticking. Luke said to Danny, "I think the time is right for a new album."

Right and overleaf: Going down a storm at London's 02 Arena.

Ben Unfortunately, I found out in January 2014 that I had what is known as head and neck cancer. It could have been caused by a virus, or by smoking, or by a combination of the two: they don't really know.

Harry When Danny phoned to tell me that Benny had cancer, my legs nearly buckled under me. I couldn't believe it.

Danny We had everything planned out for 2014, and we had all the excitement and anticipation building to go into the studio to make a new record. Ben's news definitely pulled the rug out from underneath us. We were all taken aback and wondering "What do we do now?"

Chris It was a real shock, and nobody knew quite how to react to it. It felt unreal.

Ben My oncologist told me, if you're going to get cancer, this one – or bladder cancer – are the ones to get as they're the most easily treated. The good news was that I was given a 96 per cent chance of being cured through radiotherapy alone: then they said that if I added chemotherapy, it would add another 6 to 8 per cent to that. I thought, "Hang on, that's 104 per cent. Do I get a superpower?" The bad news was that, of all the cancers that exist, head and neck requires the most arduous treatment. The radiotherapy attacks your mouth and throat, which is a very busy junction in your body, so it affects breathing, swallowing, drinking, your saliva and your hearing.

Danny I had to make sure that everything kept moving for the band, at the same time as making sure Benny was OK. He was very stoic while he went through his treatment: there was no wailing or gnashing of teeth from him. Fortunately he has a great family,

who all rallied round him, and we did the best we could to do the same thing from our perspective.

Ben Did it hurt? Fuck yes, it hurt! The radiotherapy was very painful and I was fed through a hole in my stomach for five months. You can't use your mouth for anything other than breathing: you can't even swallow water. The whole of your mouth, throat and tongue turn into one big ulcer. I was in constant pain, so I was on constant pain medication, and consequently I was addicted to co-codamol within a month. That and nicotine are the only things any member of Thunder has ever been addicted to!

Danny My father died of cancer, and my mum had it twice and survived, so I knew what Benny was going through, and I had to manage his expectations to an extent. He was determined to get through it in five minutes and be back in the studio with us. Of course, I knew that wouldn't happen.

Ben It's an odd thing: people don't like saying the word 'cancer'. They'll say things like "I heard you had, er..." and I'll say, "Cancer. You're allowed to say the word." What's also interesting is that older people don't like to say the word, but younger people aren't afraid to use it as more people survive cancer nowadays than don't. For our generation and the ones above us, cancer used to be a death sentence: there was no doubt about it. But that's all changed now: it's a remarkable achievement.

Chris It was different in the studio without Ben – not just musically but also with his personality. He brings a lot to everything we do.

Ben When I was ill, I didn't give a fuck about anything: I basically went into existence mode. I couldn't

watch TV, I couldn't read – I was too ill to do anything but lie in bed. I was very confident that I was going to be OK after the treatment, so I didn't feel any fear. At every stage they told me what was going to happen and how I was going to feel, and they were right on the button, with no bullshit. The NHS staff were exceptional; I gave them a credit on the *Wonder Days* album. I also wrote to the head nurse at Guy's Hospital afterwards and told her that her team had been amazing.

Harry I knew Ben would get through it: he's such a positive person.

Ben Cancer treatment really kicks you hard when you're already down, and is a long, arduous process, but I did manage to pull a few positives out of it. I'm now fitter and healthier than I've been in a long time, and I prefer the way I look. Luke summed it up when he said, "You've had a reboot." A new look with short hair was a bit of a shock at first, because I'd had long hair since I was seven, but it's a lot less grief.

Before I went into the treatment my sister put me on a super-strict diet, with lots of raw vegetables and nothing unhealthy whatsoever. This gave my body a chance to deal with the toxic chemicals and radiotherapy treatment without adding anything else myself. I still eat that stuff now, although I wasn't a fan of junk food anyway. I can't eat bread any more, as my salivary glands don't work so well after the treatment.

Danny was the intermediary between the band and me. He came round one day to see me and was amazed at how good I looked. The skin on my face had pretty much renewed, due to the cream given to me to counteract the side effects of the radiotherapy. He couldn't believe it.

A NEW LOOK WITH SHORT HAIR WAS A BIT OF A SHOCK AT FIRST, BECAUSE I'D HAD LONG HAIR SINCE I WAS SEVEN, BUT IT'S A LOT LESS GRIEF.

Danny While Benny was recovering, our thinking was that you can't just trade on your past and play a greatest hits set every night, so you need to make new music from time to time. And if you're going to make a new album, it needs to be a great one. That was our logic.

Luke We had the means to make a new record ourselves, but we decided to take the independent label route again. Having been down the self-releasing road through the Noughties, we realised that it was time to take the international side more seriously, which is very difficult to do yourselves. If you go with a label with an infrastructure in place, that becomes easier, although at the same time you relinquish a little bit of control. Not creative control, I hasten to add. It was the right thing to do in the end.

Wonder Days is the best album we've ever made, and the most complete from my point of view. The problem with a lot of bands of our age is nostalgia: a lot of them go out and play all of their first album, or all of their second album. That's never going to happen with us. When you do that, you lose currency. In the shows we did last year in Germany, we played eight songs from the new record, which was amazing. And they liked it, so we must be doing something right. The album came out on February 16, 2015.

Right and overleaf: The *Wonder Days* session at Rockfield in 2014.

Above, right and overleaf: The *Wonder Days* cover
shoot in Hackney, London in November 2014.

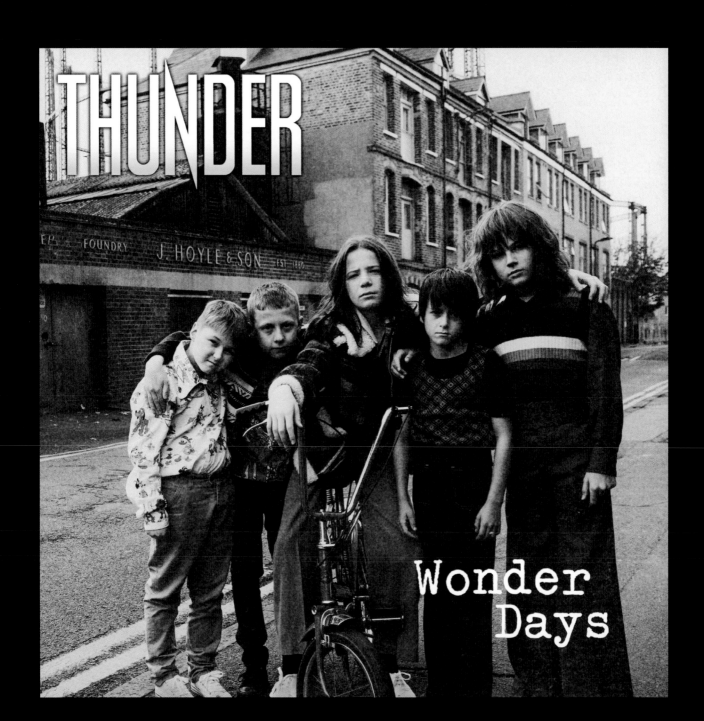

WONDER DAYS

SONG BY SONG BY LUKE MORLEY

Wonder Days

I had the musical idea for this for some time, but couldn't find a lyrical hook to hang it on. As sometimes happens, I woke up in the middle of the night with the chorus melody in my head so I got out of bed, picked up a guitar and the rest was easy! Looking back, I did enjoy being a teenager in the Seventies. I think it was a lot easier for kids then.

The Thing I Want

Uncomplicated lust. A trace of the Stones here and there.

The Rain

I read an article about the dust bowl farmers during the American Depression, and imagined myself as an Irish immigrant struggling to cope in the Thirties. It brought to mind my grandad, who came over here from Ireland to find his fortune many years ago. Songwriting takes you to strange places sometimes. This song was my debut as a mandolin player!

Black Water

This song was co-written with Lynne Jackaman, and in fact was initially written for Lynne, so when I thought it might be good for Thunder, the lyric had to be changed from a female to a male perspective. It's all about a fairly unpleasant gigolo.

The Prophet

Simon bloody Cowell! How often can one man be on television before it's too much? I think it's very unhealthy for one man to have as much influence over the kind of music we see and hear on radio and television, let alone all the celebrity drivel it spawns.

Resurrection Day

This song went through many rewrites, mainly lyrically. It was 'Graduation Day', which was too American, then it was 'Election Day', which was too pretentious. It wasn't until I was thinking about Benny being ill and trying to be positive about it that the idea of seeing light at the end of the tunnel gave the song the right thrust.

Chasing Shadows

A song written about songwriting. Always a good call when you can't think of anything else!

Broken

This song was written initially on guitar but ended up on the piano, probably because I was teaching myself at the time. I still am! I really like this recording as it's not over-produced, which is always a temptation with this kind of song.

When The Music Played

Continuing the theme of 'Wonder Days', this looks back at my early teens and specifically my relationship with music then and since. It's definitely a very different business now – and not in a good way.

Serpentine

This song was written about a good friend of the band who works in 'personal services'. She is a lot of fun and doesn't bite – unless you ask nicely, of course.

I Love The Weekend

The last song written for the album. No-nonsense, straight-ahead rock'n'roll.

Danny I've known Paul Anthony from Planet Rock for ages, and he asked me and Luke if we'd prerecord a show for New Year's Eve 2014, which we did, and after that the head honcho there, Ric Blaxill – who I knew vaguely from *Top Of The Pops* years ago – asked me to go for a beer with him. We've always done bits and bobs for Planet Rock, so it seemed natural to go and talk to him, and he asked me if I'd like to present my own radio show. I said yes, although I had no idea how to do it, and he said they would help me with all the techie stuff. But it's been great, and it's doing really well, which is amazing considering I'm just talking cobblers – and I get to play Thunder songs every week too, so that's a win–win in my book.

Luke I'm proud of the fact that we've survived many incarnations of the music industry, using our wits and our ability. I'm also proud of the fact that we're still friends. I'm very proud of how good the band is as a live act. People leave the building smiling after our shows, even at times when our music has been uncool. And I'm very proud of the fact that we've managed to remain largely decent human beings. In some ways, that's our greatest achievement. Largely decent, not entirely!

Harry A lot of our contemporaries haven't made it this far: they've split up, or just suffered bad luck. Maybe we're better than most of them were? I don't know. I know we have good songs, though. It's a great time to be

in Thunder. We're flying high – but we fucking deserve it, believe me. We've worked hard for this.

Luke Without meaning to sound cheesy, all the human things are important. You do your best, you live with the disappointments and you traverse the peaks and the pitfalls. We've been very lucky to have had a career for 26 years and counting. Lots of bands don't come close to that.

Rod: The Nineties affected a lot of rock bands: it affected Maiden to an extent, with the arrival of grunge and all the Seattle stuff. Different fashions, different attitudes: that's bound to have an effect. But Thunder are doing really well again, and they're playing arenas, and deservedly so.

Ben We have a cottage industry where we all multitask. Danny's the manager, I'm the engineer, Luke's the MD, Chris is the designer... if only Harry were a publicist, we'd have the whole thing covered! We can take an album to mastering stage without any intervention. Not many bands can do that. And we don't get caught up in our own importance. After all, we're basically the court jesters, aren't we?

We're very privileged to be where we are. I had an epiphany a good few years ago when we were in Tokyo. We'd had a brilliant show the night before, and we'd travelled on the bullet train – which is a wonderful way to travel. We were being met by a line of chauffeured

cars and being driven to the gig. It was a beautiful sunny day, and walking to our car I turned to Danny and said, "Life's pretty good, isn't it?" and he said, "Yes it is..."

Harry We've weathered a few storms, but since we've been back, our profile has gone up and up. There's still more to do, though, and I can't wait to do it.

Chris Thunder always has been, and continues to be, the easiest band I've ever worked with. I think this is what has contributed to the longevity and popularity that the band enjoys. And I have a very strange feeling that perhaps the best is yet to come...

Danny We're having a great time, Luke's writing some cracking tunes, my voice is still there, and we seem to be getting better every time we play. I'm very conscious of the fact that we're getting older, so we're running out of time to achieve our true potential – which in some ways is good, because it makes every decision really important. Our star seems to be in the ascendant again, but there's a lot more to do yet, so provided we stay healthy and physically capable, and we're enjoying it, I think we'll be around for a wee while yet.

Luke Nothing changes, really. When we get together in Thunder, we revert to our teenage selves. It's as if we never grew up – and I hope we never do!

> " NOTHING CHANGES, REALLY. WHEN WE GET TOGETHER IN THUNDER, WE REVERT TO OUR TEENAGE SELVES. IT'S AS IF WE NEVER GREW UP – AND I HOPE WE NEVER DO! "

Previous pages: Wonder nights on the *Wonder Days* tour.
Above right: A Gibson charity acoustic show in January 2016. We played at the 100 Club the same night.
Below right: Danny spins the plates at Planet Rock in July 2016.
Overleaf: Still doing what we do best. Live at the Ramblin' Man Fair on July 24, 2016.